hello universe,

It's Me

How I Scheduled a Breakdown,
and Manifested a New Life
(and How You Can, Too)

By Deepika Sandhu

The Akipeed Company
Vancouver · Los Angeles · London · San Francisco

TABLE OF CONTENTS

HELLO UNIVERSE, IT'S ME

AUTHOR'S NOTE

This is my story the way I experienced it. It is a book of reflection and inspiration. Some names, characteristics and places have been changed. Some events have been condensed, others have been omitted, dialogue has been reconstructed. Those who know me may view my story differently. And that, my friends, is the magic of life.

HELLO UNIVERSE, IT'S ME

INTRODUCTION

Curious yet highly skeptical is how I would best describe my relationship with the spiritual realm. Perhaps conflicted is a better word. My fact-checking, checklist-making, to-do-list crossing, highly logical, work hard, achieve, achieve, achieve brain could not fully embrace anything that I didn't see, touch, feel, or hear for myself. If it wasn't logical, it simply wasn't something my brain could absorb.

Yet, despite all my skepticism and all my desire to move forward with logic, there was a part of me that was always intrigued by the idea of a force greater than us guiding, directing and orchestrating this life. That curiosity led me to people, places and realms that could shed light on this life force, albeit with a healthy dose of skepticism.

Palm reading fascinated me in my early teen years. In college, it was about astrology and how the movement or position of planets gave insights into our lives. In my mid-twenties I learned to love yoga. The physical and mental awareness that yoga brought was a welcome addition as I navigated my new, stressful, and demanding professional world. In my thirties, psychics or people who had premonitions about the future enticed me. It stemmed from the buildup of dissatisfaction in my life or a misalignment with what I thought life would feel like when I seemingly had it all. When life got most desperate, I turned to people who, through their insights, premonitions and intuition, helped to reconcile the struggle I felt about where I was in my life. Yet it never fully resonated. None of it. It was intriguing but not meaningful. It was a form of entertainment. It was not something that made me change behaviors or beliefs about my life or the way I lived.

Now in my forties, I realize that searching outside of myself for the answers to my struggles was never necessary. The palm reading, the astrologers, the psychics, the mediums and all those people and places outside of myself that I went to for meaning or insight were just gateways to realize that the answers I sought were not out there somewhere. They were inside of me. I didn't need a fancy guru. I didn't need a plane ticket to India. I just needed to cultivate a relationship with myself. I needed to trust my intuition, to see *(really see)* the signs and messages that life was presenting to me in plain sight. I needed to operate as my higher self, my better self, my more aligned, aware, and knowing self in order to really see and hear all that the Universe wanted for me.

All of this took time, but once I was able to harness the energy around me and raise myself up, I could hear the various ways our world speaks to us and the way our soul speaks to us. I could start to clearly see the answers that eluded me for so long. I started to live the life I was meant to live.

This is my story of how I learned to operate from a place of positive energy, how I learned to trust my own intuition, how I cultivated my connection with the world around me, how I began to see the magic within myself and align to my higher purpose to live an inspired life. I will take you on my journey and as I do, I will show you how you can harness the energy, raise your vibration, and manifest the life you desire. No matter where you are in your life, I hope you will be able to see you have everything within yourself to make the shifts you need to live the life you are meant to live. You just need to be open. You just need to take the steps.

The Universe and I are here to help.

Let's get started.

HOW TO USE THIS BOOK

My hope is this book makes spirituality accessible to you — that you see through my own story how you can cultivate a relationship with the Universe in any way that works for you. That these words create gentle bells within you that allow you to embark on the path to becoming your truest self. I hope to show that you don't (necessarily) need exotic travels, worship of foreign deities, or anything of that sort to find what is deeply rooted within you. My journey was done right in my home with a whole lotta introspection and by actively cultivating my own awareness that (finally) allowed me to see what was staring at me in the face.

Each chapter starts with a Letter to the Universe. For me, the Universe represents the Eternal, the Omnipresent, the Divine. For you, it may be God, The Holy Spirit, the Essence, the Source, the Creator. Whatever the label, just know that this is the ever-present, larger-than-this-life source, the energy that is our ultimate truth. It is the One with whom I am always trying to connect to help guide me and unlock the truth within. I cultivated a relationship with the Universe as a means of transcending the life I was living and to connect to all that is beyond this physical realm.

The entries included here are inspired by my actual journal during this period of my life. I follow each entry with more of my personal story and then end each chapter with a Hello Friend letter. You are the friend. You are the one I am speaking to. You are the one that I hope has a gazillion beautiful "a-ha" moments.

You are the one that can find your truest self. These letters to you are a small offering of what may help get you there. Through mantras, affirmation, exercise, and meditation, I will show you how to incorporate spiritual practices into your everyday life. These are the tiny steps that you can take to move in the direction of the truest version of you.

More than anything, I hope these insights into my life, my story and how it can connect to your own story helps you see that your story matters, the way you navigate your life matters and finding who you are meant to be and what you are meant to offer this world matters, too. I see you. Soon enough you will see you, too.

HELLO UNIVERSE, IT'S ME

SECTION 1: SEEING ME
(AND HOW YOU CAN SEE YOU TOO)

HELLO UNIVERSE, IT'S ME

CHAPTER 1

Hello Universe,

You are persistent.

Now that I have gotten to know you, I realize You have been there all along. I just didn't notice You. You were the man that stopped me in my tracks as I raced to work to give me a compliment. You were the adorable fluffy dog with the big loving eyes that crossed my path on my evening walk. You were the spark in my gut when I did something that made me feel alive. For the fleeting seconds when these instances occurred, I sensed someone or something was trying to catch my attention, but I just ignored the flares You were giving off. I didn't have the awareness to realize that was You. I was so wrapped up in my brain and in living my supposedly amazing life that I really didn't give You more than a passing thought.

I was so darn busy trying to cross things off my checklist. You know that checklist. I am sure every time You saw me make one and cross something off, You just laughed. You knew all my checklists were going to backfire one day, didn't you? Of course You did. Well, thanks for letting me do what I needed to do to realize I didn't need to do it anymore.

I really believed that all those checklists were going to work. I was too naïve to know any different. I was busy studying hard at college trying to get great grades so I could land a great job. I was busy working that corporate job so I could climb the ladder of success and get the next promotion and then the next one after that. I was busy dating like it was a professional sport, trying to find Prince Charming. I was busy driving my fun sports car, going to swanky restaurants, flying away on fancy vacations, and posting about it on the most popular social media of the day. I was meeting friends for cappuccinos during the day and martinis at night. I was buying fun purses, cute clothes, and lots of shoes (so many shoes) as if all that stuff was going to get me wherever I needed to be. Just constantly doing, doing, doing.

You knew all along that my checklist-making would fail me and You let me fail. I guess that was necessary to get me where I needed to be. You knew, and I had to find out, that none of my checklists said, "Be Happy" or "Live Your Highest Purpose" or "Align with Your Soul." Nope, none of them said that. If someone had mistakenly put that on one of my checklists back then, I would have scoffed! It wouldn't have meant a thing to me. Instead I had to wake up and realize that after years and years of checking all the boxes, after getting everything I supposedly thought I needed, something very large was missing.

I thought I had crossed the finish line on life and everything was smooth sailing from here. I mean, I had the strong academic record, the amazing career, I got married, I bought a house, I had a child, I was living what I thought was an amazing life.

I was running through it all. As if, the faster I ran, the more I did, the more I posted about what I was doing, the faster

I checked the boxes, the better my life would be. Kinda like sprinting your way through a marathon. Running, running, running as fast as I could, as long as I could, and then collapsing on that finish line from exhaustion to realize that instead of being somewhere or having achieved something, I was really nowhere at all.

I was conditioned to be a success addict. Every step I took was about achieving the next external measure of success. My parents ingrained this in me early. Personal satisfaction and happiness could only emerge as you checked the boxes. As a kid this was about good grades, doing my homework, being nice to guests as they came over, dressing up perfectly so people would admire us and all those accomplishments we were racking up. My checklist was all about achievement. None of it had anything to do with happiness.

Yet, I wasn't happy. My achievements were not enough. My house full of HGTV-worthy decor was not enough. My closets full of stylish clothes were not enough. That beautiful, happy, healthy kid. Wasn't she enough? Was I selfish and ungrateful for realizing all that list-checking, all the accomplishments, all that doing simply didn't get me where I needed to go? Others looked at my world with envy. They not only saw a full life, they saw one that was overflowing with goodness. They saw the material things, the career accomplishments, the family, the bright smiles posted on social media and thought she has it all. But what I realized is all that sprinting through my life landed me nowhere at all. I was overworked, exhausted, depleted, and downright sad. That was the wakeup call.

It wasn't as if this realization came out of nowhere. You were pretty good about dropping hints along the way that something wasn't right. Whenever I was alone with my thoughts or having an unexpected quiet moment, a sinking feeling would emerge that all of this wasn't doing what I thought it was meant to. But I wouldn't let myself sit with those nanoseconds of realization. I was excellent at ignoring You and moving past those feelings as quickly as humanly possible. Yet it persisted. It nagged and kept right on nagging, demanding, jumping up and down for my attention like a needy toddler. I simply couldn't ignore it anymore. My life was off. I needed to re-think what I was doing. I needed to get things straight. I needed to figure out why everything I thought I wanted and needed was no longer what I wanted or needed.

So I scheduled a breakdown.

Always,
Me

We are human beings — not human doings. Yet we exist in a constant cycle of doing. It gets ingrained in us early. Kids today are busier than ever before. As a parent of a school-aged child, I should know. My kid goes to ballet, art, swim, and piano classes all in one week and she is the least scheduled kid in her class. Our kids are doers because we as parents are a generation of doers. It started early for us, too. We were conditioned that the more you do in high school, like debate club, cheerleading, track, starting a volunteer society plus succeeding at academics, opens the door to University. There we were conditioned to do, do, do even more, whether that was socializing more — more parties, more beer, more dates, more adventures — or learning more — double majors, double minors, study abroad, extra classes.

It doesn't end at college. The rest of our real lives are all about go, go, go. About achieving. Succeeding. How much do you make? What car do you drive? How many dating apps you are on? How many boyfriends? Hookups? Did you get your steps in? Did you keep your carbs in check? You name it. We count it and keep track of it. We are a scorecard society and I was actively taking score not only of myself but of others. The more I did, the more likes, clicks and comments I racked up, meant I was well perceived, which further meant I must be better at all the doing than anyone else or at least keeping up with what everyone else was doing.

My scorecard was full. I was winning at the game of life. If I was in a giant football stadium the big monitors over the field would be flashing in bold, capital letters "YOU ARE KILLING IT!" I was not only killing it. It was killing me.

I had no reason to question it. The life I was living seemed to be similar to the way others around me were living too. All the working mommas at the office and all the working mommas on my favorite TV shows, movies and social media seemed to be doing the same thing. They were all juggling kids, careers, husbands and making it look effortless. So why shouldn't I? Yet if I ever did stumble upon a moment of quiet while taking a walk alone or sitting in my backyard with a cup of coffee, I could literally hear my exhausted self ask: *Why doesn't this feel right? Why do I feel like an imposter in the life I thought I wanted?*

Take the night before my daughter's first birthday. I was in a mad rush to put her to sleep. We were doing our usual nighttime routine in her room — the elephant-themed room with shades of grey, white and touches of orange. A year ago, we didn't know if our baby was going to be a boy or girl so the room was designed in neutral tones. The room was a labor of love. My mom made her curtains by hand. My aunt handstitched beautiful pillows for the cozy chair in the corner. My brother and sister painted her room. My husband and my brother assembled the Ikea dresser, which took an absurdly long time to put together. There was so much love put into this space that our new baby would enjoy for so many years to come.

Now she was on the eve of her first birthday. Instead of sitting in awe of that, I was rushing her to bed hoping she would go to bed faster tonight than other nights (no luck there). I needed her to sleep so I could finish the prep for her party. There were more handmade decorations to assemble. Little cowgirl hats and bandanas that needed to be displayed perfectly. The chalkboard signs needed their wittily worded cowgirl phrases to be perfectly written on. There were goodie bags to pack. The pink bags needed their custom sticker with my daughter's name to be perfectly positioned on each one. And don't forget the cute bow with the curling ribbon! I needed to get that ribbon ready for 30 goodie bags. I had hours more of prep in front of me and my kid had no plans of sleeping. Once she did finally sleep, I got to work. It was after midnight before I finished. As I sat amidst my decorations, the ribbon, the pink bags, the mini cowgirl hats, a wave of total and complete exhaustion washed over me.

Why did I stay up perfecting Pinterest-worthy decorations for my daughter's first birthday? I mean, the cowgirl-themed party was a dream with pink cowgirl hats, professional grillers, a petting zoo, a magician, perfectly wrapped party favors. It was a great party. But why? Why did I do this? I exhausted myself putting this party together while trying to make it look effortless. The party was well received and the compliments from the guests flowed, but was any of it really necessary?

My daughter will surely never remember her first birthday. She fell asleep in the middle of the party and missed the petting zoo. We had to coax her awake to cut the cake. Yes, I have some wonderful photographs from the event and it was fun, but I wonder why time after time I worked tirelessly to host elaborate parties, dinners and Thanksgiving celebrations. Why was I wanting or thinking I needed to do these things when I had so little time? Why was I staying up late, after a full and exhausting day at work, to make party favors, or seating cards or decorations of one kind or another when I could have been sleeping, resting, attending to my daughter or making a memory as a family that was simpler and less time-intensive?

More than even coming up with simpler parties and simpler ways to connect as a family, why was all my doing not making me feel good? In fact, I was feeling the opposite. Maybe I got a temporary high from a partygoer's compliment. Maybe I felt positive after a smile from my husband or a hug from my daughter. Yet, I couldn't reconcile in my mind why I was putting forth so much effort to make others believe my cowgirl birthday party skills were so effortless and amazing? And if I was doing that, why was it not lifting me up further? Why was it not making me feel good? Why was it leaving me depleted, exhausted, empty?

In the middle of the party, as kids were running around, as the jovial guy cooking up burgers on the BBQ cracked jokes, as friends and family enjoyed cold drinks in the bright sunshine of our background, I looked around at all the faces in the room. I was giving off my fake smile in every direction. Yet all I could feel was an overwhelming sense of fatigue. Instead of being happy about the fun people seemed to be having, I was faking my own enthusiasm to mask the way I really felt. But that's what I did. That was normal for me — to do so much all the time and to not really enjoy any of that doing at all.

This went on for years. Running my way through life. Rushing to get ready each morning. Rushing to work. Rushing my way through meetings. Rushing home each day to be with my daughter. Rushing my way through making dinner. Rushing my way through feeding my daughter, giving her bath, reading her a book. Rushing to put her to sleep so I could get back online and keep working. Then waking up the next day to do it all again. Through all that rushing, I felt lost. On the outside of my life, everything looked amazing. It was a high-like social media situation. But I was lost, beyond lost, on the inside.

It all culminated when my husband had to be out of town for 10 days. At the time, we were the owners of a small neighborhood market. It was a cute little historic building in an older part of town that we hoped would be our entry into successful small business ownership. He was proud to own this small shop that employed seven people and was a gathering point for many in the community. It was his pet project. His job. His domain.

When he left for 10 days it was no small feat to keep everything afloat. I already had a full-time demanding job working more than 50 hours a week. The nanny (the most lovely, caring, attentive woman on the planet) also had a vacation planned for the same days to visit her children. She hadn't taken a vacation for more than a year, so I didn't have the heart to ask her to reschedule when my husband's trip emerged. Oh, and while the husband and nanny were gone, my preschool-going daughter brought home all those germs from school and became sick. Like bad sick. So sick that she could not go to preschool. Not only did I have to figure out how to get to our market, make sure the shelves were full, make the bank deposits, and make sure the registers had enough change, I also had to stay home from my own work because my child was sick and needed the loving care of her mom. When my sick child rested, my laptop was open and I tried to stay apace with my own demanding job as much as I could before she woke up and needed my care again.

It was mid-morning on a Friday. My daughter slept well the night before and just ate a decent breakfast. Her energy level was so much better. Yesterday she was completely lethargic and spent most of the day lying in my lap. Maybe she was turning the corner today? Maybe she and I could brave the 40-minute drive, check on the market, and be back before for her afternoon nap? I had a conference call with a client to take but I could do that in the car on the way there. I hadn't showered but I could throw on a baseball cap, some lip gloss, big hoop earrings (channel my inner Jennifer Lopez), and make myself presentable. It was raining outside but not at a pace where the drive would be dangerous. I looked at the clock. I looked at my daughter. *Should we do it?* She smiled. I took that as a yes. I quickly grabbed her car toys, packed her snack bag, loaded her in the car seat, and off we went.

The drive started off incredibly pleasant. Thanks to recent rain, the rolling hills hugging the freeway were perfectly green. Cows grazed on the hills, something which always fascinated my daughter. We talked about their colors, what conversations we thought they were having with one another. And of course, our favorite activity — counting the cows all along the way. We got to about 49 before I had to hop on my conference call. My daughter was getting sleepy in the back seat (counting cows surely helped). The timing was perfect. I was feeling like my Super Mom powers were in full force. *Yes, I sure could take this call with a client, with my daughter in the backseat, while driving in the rain all the way to our market. Super Momma just making it work over here.* I felt like high-fiving someone, or if I were a dude I might pound my chest. But I just smiled. *I got this. Who says I can't do it all? I am doing it all right now and I am doing it all incredibly well if I do say so myself. I can handle it all. And I make it look easy. Oh yeah, sooooo in control of this situation.* That feeling didn't last more than five minutes.

As I was listening to my client describe their latest issue that required my attention, my daughter softly cried out *"Momma"* in a sweet yet incredibly weak way. I looked in my rear-view mirror and heard the dreaded sound no mother wants to hear — *"BLLEAAHH"*. My daughter vomited all over herself and the backseat. Super Momma mode done. I pulled over, abruptly ended the call with the client, and began cleaning up the giant mess of vomit while comforting my daughter, who was now crying. Does Jennifer Lopez have days like this too?

I barely got through those 10 days. I was exhausted. I was sleep-deprived (my preschooler was never a good sleeper). I was overworked. I was drained. Every ounce of my being was exhausted by all that I had to take on. Sure, I could smile and say I handled it. But this was one time when handling it was too exhausting to bear.

The grand finale was picking up my husband from the airport. I managed to shower that day. Even put on a bit of makeup. I was relieved to have him home not necessarily for his company (by this point in our marriage I found him to be unenthusiastic, overly critical, and disinterested in the life we had) but more for the sheer fact that I was exhausted from doing his job, my job, and caring for a sick kid. I was ready for another adult in the home so things could get back to normal, whatever that meant.

I pulled up to the curb at baggage claim, my husband hopped in and shouted, *"Go, go, go"* as he pounded the dashboard of the car. There was no kiss. No *"Hello, Honey."* No warm embrace. Just him wanting me to move my car as fast as possible to not inconvenience anyone behind us. Why this surprised me as it did, I do not know. He had never been one for loving gestures. There was never much love between us. Even when we dated, it was more of a flirtatious friendship than love. I thought friendship was sufficient for marriage. I was wrong.

I looked at him in disbelief. He was gone for 10 days. I kept everything afloat and I couldn't even get a hello from him. In that moment, he was more concerned about us blocking others from picking up their loved ones on the curb by baggage claim than even muttering hello to his supposed loved one. I was flabbergasted. I just stared at him for what felt like forever. He looked at me pointed ahead and said, *"Come on, let's go!"* There wasn't much talking in the car, although my mind was talking nonstop: *Are you kidding me? Did that just really happen? Am I not even worthy of a proper embrace? Am I not even worthy of a moment of gratitude for picking you up? I am your wife. Appreciate me! Say you love me! Is this really all you can do? Just say "let's go?" Is that it? You treat perfect strangers better than this.*

Maybe he was tired from a long flight. Maybe I was being unreasonable for thinking he would understand or even be aware of how difficult the last 10 days had been. I don't know. But what I did know in that moment, is that something needed to change.

Those 10 days were perfectly orchestrated by the Universe. I needed a do-over. I needed a Control+Alt+Delete on my life. I needed a reboot. I needed to throw all those checklists out the window. I needed to drop-kick the to-do list. I needed to pound the crap out of the scorecard and break it into a million pieces. I needed to stop feeling like I needed to or even could do it all. I needed an "I Dream of Jeannie" head nod to shake things up and get this all back on track.

I desperately needed to stop doing. No more. No more rushing. No more trying to be perfect. No more trying to get to what is next. No more achieving. No more succeeding, please. No more taking on more and more and more. I was already beyond capacity. I needed a break. I desperately needed to figure out how to be a human being and not be a human doing. We weren't put on this earth to do, do, do. We were put on this earth to be. Just be. So it was time for me to be. No more doing. Way more being.

In that moment, driving my husband home from the airport, I knew without question that my life no longer resembled anything that was authentic or real to me in any way. I was an imposter. I was someone I no longer recognized in a life that I no longer wanted to be a part of.

I needed to make a change.

Hello Friend,

Have you felt like this before? You took on so much. One small thing here. One big thing there. One after another. It just piled up. More drop-offs. More carpools. More kid's parties. More work. More deadlines. More family gatherings. More. More. More. All the while feeling pressure to do all of it with a smile, gracefully, without complaining. After all, isn't this what superwomen are supposed to do? Then there is a moment when you just can't take on anymore. You break down. You give up. You throw in the towel. You have had enough.

All the seemingly small incidents and challenges you have been dealing with suddenly becomes significant enough to create the sensation that something needs to change. It could be a physical change such as deciding to say no to something or stepping out of a difficult situation. Other times, the change is more subtle, as it was for me: more of a recognition that while you may not have the answers right this second, you need to go deep within yourself to see what needs to change to correct course.

But what I really want you to know, Friend, is this is all okay. It's okay to question the things happening in your life. It is okay to re-evaluate where you are and what you are doing. It's okay if the things meant to make you happy, that you have worked hard to achieve or acquire, give you no joy. It's okay to cry. To realize your truest self, you must acknowledge how you feel in your core, in your essence, in your soul.

Try This

Think back to the last time you felt exhausted or overwhelmed by life. What triggered that moment? Take a few minutes to close your eyes and go back to that place. How were you feeling? Why were those feelings emerging? How did you get past it? Did you get past it? Allow yourself to reflect on what happened. As you sit with this, is there anything coming up for you? Do you see a pattern that needs to break? Do you see a lesson you were meant to gain in that moment? Do you see triggers that you can work to prevent?

I believe when we feel that exhausted, that tired, that overwhelmed, it is the way the Universe is trying to get our attention. The Universe does interesting things to get our attention. Sometimes big things. Sometimes small. Just watch and see.

Always,
Me

HELLO UNIVERSE, IT'S ME

CHAPTER 2

Hello Universe,

*You knew that was going to happen, didn't you? You knew
I would be this upset. You knew I would be so upset that
my head would spin and I wouldn't even be able to bring
myself to get in bed and put the day behind me. Instead,
I am sitting in my closet, using the light of my cell phone
to write to You. He is sound asleep. He got home from the
airport, had something to eat and just passed out. I suppose
I would be tired too after a long flight. Maybe I shouldn't
be so upset about what happened today? Yet it seems You
perfectly orchestrated a set of circumstances that on its
surface is seemingly inconsequential but is actually highly
consequential to me. Why?!*

*I keep trying to intellectualize it. Make sense of it. Try to
explain it. But this time, unlike all the times before, I can't
do it. My husband had never been very expressive or
complimentary. That was true when we were dating — and
it has been true through the seven years of our marriage.
So why am I expecting or wanting him to be communicative
and affectionate now? Just like so many women out there, I
never gave up hope that it could get better. That he could be
different. That he could love me more. That our relationship
could fulfill me more. But today at the airport, that hope of it*

becoming better just shattered. Now I am sitting in the corner of my closet in my trashy housewife pajamas (the ripped ones that I should have thrown out eons ago, but are still so comfortable that I keep wearing them) with my journal, my cell phone and a cup of hot chocolate doing the ugly, sobbing cry while my daughter and husband sleep.

When I step back and analyze it (because let's face it, that is all I am doing — on turbo speed), maybe it isn't a big deal. Maybe he doesn't know how hard the last 10 days have been? I haven't spoken to him much while he was away. Maybe I am expecting him to realize something that isn't obvious?

But then again, this has nothing to do with him. This has everything to do with me, doesn't it? The moment in the car at the airport, that was a sign, wasn't it? It was your way of sending me a message. I just want you to know, Universe, I heard this one loud and clear. I know in the past You have sent me a wink, a sign, a whisper and it completely passed me by. Even if I recognized it was from You, I didn't know what to make of it and nudged it off. Well, don't worry, Universe: I got this one and I am committed to making a change. Please give me the strength to figure out how to do it.

Let's figure it out together.

Always,
Me

Hitting a wall. Breaking down. Downward spiral. Hitting the fan. Nervous breakdown. Unglued. Unhinged. It is the moment where we are no longer able to operate the way in which we did previously. Life overwhelms us in such a way that a seemingly uncontrolled reaction bubbles up from deep within ourselves. We lash out. We get angry. We cry. We feel deep pain. It seems different than our normal day-to-day behaviors — and, like so much in our society, if it is different, then it must be bad, wrong, unnecessary.

Rather than view the uncontrolled outburst or raw emotions as a negative, I see them as the ultimate act of awareness. A breakdown is a pause, a reset, a rebalancing. Instead of a moment where you cry it out on the couch with a tub of ice cream `a-la Bridget Jones or start throwing your living-room décor at the wall (or your love interest) like Scarlett O'Hara in *Gone with the Wind* (all of which can feel thoroughly satisfying in the moment), why can we not see hitting a wall as a triumph? It is a gift of presence. It is an example of being completely in the moment and fully aware of the intensity of the feelings that you are experiencing. It is a beautiful and sometimes painful experience to realize that you are operating in a way that no longer feels right.

That moment in the car picking up my husband from the airport was no more than 60 seconds. I experienced it in slow motion, less as a participant and more of a spectator watching from above. I was elevated out of the car, watching a scene unfold beneath me: a perfect Oscar-worthy scene where the moviegoer feels the actress's raw emotions exactly as her character is experiencing them. In that moment, I was completely aware. I could feel my heart clench, then sink. I could feel the tears welling behind my eyes. I could feel my neck struggling to control my voice from rising in an angry outburst. I could feel my face forcibly keeping a smile. I could feel the deep disappointment in my gut. I was physically experiencing my defeat in a way that was raw, authentic, and painful. It was so profound that it changed everything.

It was my wakeup call. It was my breakdown. It was my pivotal moment. It was the prelude to a complete reset and rebalance. Yet having the life that I had, the responsibilities that I had — to my family, to my job, to the carpool — I couldn't just runaway. Heck, I couldn't even take a weekend to cry it out on the couch. I couldn't pack up and run off to my mom's house. I couldn't go from doing absolutely everything to doing absolutely nothing to figure it all out. I just couldn't. All I could do was sit in my closet, cry, and do what I do best — make a plan. I decided to schedule a breakdown.

This was pretty much the only way my type-A brain could allow a much-needed restart to take place. Sitting on the floor of my closet, in the dark, surrounded by my handbags, clothes, shoes, I reached for my iPhone through my tears, pulled up my calendar and looked at the dates. I decided June was the right time for the breakdown. Problem was it was only January. I had to get through five months of my life before I gave myself permission to have a breakdown.

I didn't have the luxury that Elizabeth Gilbert had in *Eat, Pray, Love*: I couldn't just extract myself from my world in the hopes of finding myself. I couldn't leave behind the job, my kid and all my responsibilities. The only choice left was to find space within the confines of my life to break down. To take time from my day-to-day to find me. To take time to slowly gather up the courage to do whatever was needed to set myself on the right path to being the most authentic version of myself. The version that didn't betray myself by being in a loveless marriage. The version of myself that didn't make myself small so my husband could feel big. The version of myself that I once was but for some reason forgot or left behind. It was time to find me again. And if that needed to be scheduled to happen five months from now, then so be it.

Just knowing there was a time coming when I would be able to pause, reflect and re-balance my life was liberating. I had something to anticipate. There was a time coming when things would change. This allowed me to find some peace as I operated in my do, do, *do* world. I didn't stop working hard. I didn't stop hustling. I was still rushing around doing the gazillion things I had to get done every day. But slowly I let a few things slide off that to-do list. I took on slightly less. I said no to social obligations here and there. I stopped hosting parties and dinners for friends and family. I took on fewer new clients. I stopped posting on Facebook. I no longer cared how my life looked to others. I attempted to find the tiny crevasses in my life to allow that restart — even if I had no idea how it would all come together. And when a day did overwhelm me, I would gently remind myself that my breakdown was coming and that alone would lift the stress just a tiny little bit.

To make my pending breakdown palatable to those around me and not raise any alarm bells with friends and family that something was wrong, I started telling those near and dear to me that after five years of employment, my company offered a four-week sabbatical (which it, and most other companies, did not offer). To those at work, I just said I was taking four weeks off for my 40th birthday: one to celebrate each decade. This made me sound empowered and focused. They had no idea the "sabbatical" was just a mask for a total and complete life reset.

Planning being my forte, I carefully formulated what time away from my normal daily life would look like. While it might have been nice to jet off to some exotic location, with a small child at home that version of discovering myself didn't seem possible, or frankly that interesting, as I had traveled quite a bit. I didn't need an escape to some fancy, faraway destination. I wanted to re-examine my life by being right here in it. I planned a staycation of sorts with short weekend trips here and there where it was feasible for my husband to care for our daughter on his own.

The process of planning and anticipating this breakdown created tiny shifts that were the start of something magnificent.

Hello Friend,

If you are anything like me, there have been many times in your life when you wanted to just cry it out. You wanted to throw something. You wanted to devour that tub of ice cream. Heck, you may be feeling like doing that right this second. Well, I want you to know that it is completely and totally okay. I give you full permission to eat whatever, throw whatever, and experience whatever emotions come to you.

When you are done eating, crying, throwing, and experiencing that raw emotion, I want you to experience something else. I want you to pause. Take a deep breath. I want you to just be fully present in what may feel like a terrible, messy, excruciating moment.

The Universe presented you this raw cadre of emotions to not pull you down into some negative space but rather to lift you up. You are not spinning or falling into something that is bad, dark, deep and terrible. When we experience a breakdown, we are being asked to lift up, to elevate, to hear and experience what the Universe is trying to tell us. The Universe had to shake us, make us mad, make us sad or scare us to get our attention. But now that it has our attention, we can listen, we can ask. What I am meant to know from this?

How you choose to answer that question is completely up to you. For me, it was scheduling several weeks for reflection. I completely recognize that isn't feasible for everyone. But ask yourself are there ways you can slow down and tune into *yourself to understand why all these emotions came up? Can you create tiny crevasses in your own life for new insights and new energy to seep in? Can you find ways to separate from all the doing so you can try just being a bit more?*

If you are cynical, you may be asking yourself, "Why? What's the point? Nothing is going to change anyway." If you are more open and receptive in this moment, you may be saying to yourself, "Yes — let's start!" Wherever you are on this spectrum, I want you to tune into how this will feel when you give yourself space to just be.

Have you ever played the Bridal Shower Gum Game? It's the one where you ask the bride questions about the groom. If she gets the answer right, everyone cheers. But if she gets any wrong, she has to place a piece of gum in her mouth. As the bride answers more and more questions wrong, she keeps stuffing her mouth with more gum until she can't stuff another piece in her mouth and ends up spitting them all out. As she spits out all that gum, what happens? She is relieved. She can breathe again.

That's what I want for you. For that feeling of release. That feeling you may be experiencing - overwhelmed, on the edge, about to choke - to just dissipate.

Always,
Me

HELLO UNIVERSE, IT'S ME

CHAPTER 3

Hello Universe,

The shifts began the minute I looked at my calendar and determined June was the month. I was a full five months away from my scheduled breakdown, but You knew that I needed shifts to start right away, however small, if I was going to make it. You knew that I was now open and ready to start receiving tiny messages from You that could slowly penetrate my very tough, hard, and busy exterior.

The shifts are coming in the most interesting of ways! You keep presenting little messages to me in my regular everyday life. You must have done that before, but I never had the patience to see what was in plain sight. As I start to slow down and stop adding more crap to my to-do list, I am able to be more present in each day. This is allowing me to see things I was blind to before. I know what I see are messages from You. They are literally everywhere.

I can't believe I didn't notice how much You spoke to me before. I have no idea what to do with the messages or what they mean. But for now, I know when I see something or experience something and it resonates, it's You. You are the one catching my attention. You are the one making me perk up and take notice.

For this I am so thankful.

Always,
Me

When you book a tropical vacation, you start envisioning yourself on that beach, soaking in the sunshine, with your favorite frosty beverage in hand (preferably with a tiny paper umbrella) from the minute you book your flight. You are dreaming of those chocolate macadamia nuts, you can feel the sand between your toes, and just laying out under your favorite cabana. You are already shifting into a beachy mindset even though your trip may be weeks or months away.

The same is true for shifts you are trying to make in your life. Committing begins the process of letting the tiniest of changes start to seep through your being. There will be heavy lifting to do. You will need to put forth the effort. You will have to do the work. But the process of setting the intention and putting the wheels in motion creates tiny spaces within yourself to allow whatever you are shifting into to find space within yourself to grow.

Knowing that I needed the breakdown, needed to launch a giant reset of my life and was giving myself the time to do this work, however far off that may be, started to produce a sense of calm. Just the act of knowing that my pending breakdown was near felt quite soothing. I was waking up to the possibility that my life could in fact be different and this created tranquil waves unlike anything I experienced before.

I had power over my life again. I was in control. I felt victorious. The Dalai Lama, Oprah, Deepak Chopra and every other spiritual guru from San Francisco to Bhutan would give me a disparaging wag of their finger for using these words. Part of me knew I had to give up control and change the way I was experiencing this life. But I could not just drop the mic on all the planning either. I needed to move into my new place of being, but I had to do it in a way that I understood. If I wanted to remain in control and not be crying in my closet every night over how terrible my life was while I waited for my breakdown to begin, I needed to have some power over my situation. I wasn't going to go from high-powered, hyper-scheduled, super-mom, career woman, Pinterest enthusiast to legs folded on a lotus flower chanting *om* without a plan. I needed a plan!

The plan was to simply be aware that life did not have to move at the frenetic pace to which I was accustomed and, more importantly, felt expected to maintain. Step One started with letting things go. My life didn't have to be filled to the brim with activities to show how productive or how important I was. Instead, I could conscientiously reengineer my life in such a way where I slowly took on less, did less, scheduled less and in so doing I would realize how much more I had. Simply put, I started saying no.

The easiest place to start was dinner parties hosted by my husband's friends. Going involved a series of activities I didn't want to participate in — keeping my daughter up past her bedtime, making small talk with people with whom I had nothing in common, and spending time dressing up knowing all the while I would be incessantly judged for what I wore and how I looked. All of this so my husband could drink, laugh and be the life of the party. When the next dinner party came along, instead of feeling obligated to attend I suggested that my husband go on his own so he could enjoy his evening while my daughter and I could enjoy ours. He got to go out and have fun. We got to sleep on time while enjoying some much needed quiet. I thought it was a win-win. He didn't view it that way.

Slowly (and I mean really slowly) this gave way to something magical. More time in the form of seconds, minutes, and eventually hours to do nothing more than be present in my life and notice what was going on around me. Just simply noticing the everyday ordinary happenings in my day that were previously overlooked and not even acknowledged because I was too busy doing.

This relatively simple plan — say no, do less, notice more — created a sense of victory. When I found myself with a few extra seconds alone, I was no longer terrified of what being alone with my thoughts might reveal. I learned to enjoy these moments of alone time. A part of me larger than logic began to drive — and that mental victory was tremendous. In the few months leading to my sabbatical, through one tiny shift here and one tiny shift there, I showed myself that I could have power over this mind. I could have power over my schedule. I had the power to say no. I could take on less. I could start to breathe. With each of those breaths, I could change my life by creating space within myself, however tiny, for the shifts to take hold.

The shifts began instantly. They were tiny, subtle, serendipitous, and all-around lovely. I started to refer to these moments as Soul Sparks: the seemingly random signposts that appear in our regular day-to-day lives that awaken us. They are tiny hints that pop up and make us take a pause. It is the spark that makes us stop in our tracks. The spark that feels like (and is) a sign from the Universe that gives us insight into whatever may be top of mind in our lives. They are not random. They are not coincidences. These are the ways that the Divine quite literally puts up a flare, a spark that gives us a glimpse, a pause, a moment to consider how we are traversing our earthly terrain. The Soul Spark may be a confirmation to stay on the path you are on or a clue to move in a direction you are dreaming of or something in between. They are sometimes as subtle as the bird chirping outside of your window to direct your attention in a new way or as obvious as getting admitted to your first-choice graduate school. The Soul Sparks become more and more apparent when you slow life down enough to notice the signposts that are all around us.

Since my plan called for saying no, doing less, and observing more, I quite literally began to see the Soul Sparks everywhere. Just being slightly less busy, slightly less rushed, slightly less scheduled meant I could see things in my everyday life that I never saw before. Walking through a crowded sidewalk in downtown San Francisco, a flower petal would fall in my path. Driving down the same streets that I drive every day (sometimes multiple times a day) I would notice a sign off the side of the road or the shape of a tree that I never noticed before. Or on the days I commuted on the busy train, the look in someone's eye and the smell of their cologne would catch me by surprise. Instead of being too busy to notice these moments, I would literally be taken aback with the beauty and wonder it. How lightly the petal danced in the air before landing at my feet. How miraculous it was that I noticed a physical sign on the streets I traversed daily with a word on it that resonated so deeply. How the look of a perfect stranger intently gazing at my eyes caused a shiver. These moments seemed to correspond naturally to the worry, the fear, the contemplation of the moment. Each such event was a Soul Spark for me. While sometimes the message seemed definitive, others I couldn't clearly decipher. I would just take note of what appeared to be a message, file it away, and not worry about analyzing it in that moment. At some point, the meaning would be clear.

Hello Friend,

Have you ever had the experience of saying you wanted to make a change and then suddenly things started to line up to make that change a reality? For example, you decide you want to get healthy. You want to eat better, exercise more, and get healthier overall. You make a commitment to implement changes that will support this. The next day you get a text from a friend saying she can get you a gym discount. You never mentioned to her that you were looking to join a gym, but now you have a discounted membership and a friend to go with. At the gym, you strike up a conversation with someone who has a blog about nutrition. You are intrigued. You start to follow her blog and the recipes she posts. Soon after you are cooking healthy meals for your family. You are feeling better and looking better.

The same concept can work in all aspects of your life. Ask yourself this: if you could change any aspect of your life right now, what would it be? To answer this, I want you to get deeply in tune with yourself.

Try This — *One way to do this is to create an oasis, a magical and sacred space, where we can retreat and connect. To do this, find a place at home or in the backyard. It may be your closet, your bathroom or, if you are lucky, you may have a spare bedroom or a corner of your garage that you can use. You can transform this oasis in any way you want to make it truly yours. Your oasis may have candles, the lights may be dim, you may be seated, lying down, you may have a blanket or stuffed animal. Or it may be as simple as a little mat and a cushion. Keeping a journal and a pen on hand to write down thoughts that may emerge in your oasis is a good idea too. We are simply trying to create a space where you can retreat and truly hear yourself.*

Settling into your oasis, I want you to tune inward. Close your eyes, take some deep calming breaths. Once you are settled into this quiet space, ask yourself what about your life needs changing? Receive whatever bubbles up for you. Don't analyze or judge. Just write down the first few things that emerge when you consider what needs to change in your life to make things better. It could be increasing your level of physical fitness. It could be creating more boundaries in your personal relationship. It could be spending more time with your kids. Sit with the answers that are emerging and just allow this awareness to wash over you. As you emerge from this revelation, thank yourself for the insight. You may not know right now what to do with whatever surfaced, but just thank yourself for taking these moments to listen to your innermost self.

When we can hear, truly hear, what is needed to transform our lives and we begin to believe that these changes are in fact what we want, life starts magically lining up to support our desires. Just putting the desire, the intent, the hope out into the world allows the magic to happen. Sometimes it is immediate and other times a bit more gradual. The shifts may be subtle or giant. Either way, life has a way of rising to meet and support us. We must just allow it to take form.

Always.
Me

CHAPTER 4

Hello Universe,

The way You began to present people and places that give a glimpse of how transformative my scheduled breakdown will be, is nothing short of incredible. You knew I needed these little sprinkles in the months leading up to June so I would be open and receptive to all my breakdown would bring.

Like finding out my favorite yoga teacher, who I lost touch with after moving away 10 years ago, was hosting a four-day silent yoga retreat and the dates perfectly lined up with my breakdown. Like the amazing and kind woman who popped up out of nowhere to paint with me almost every day during my time off from the tiny studio in her garage. Like being invited to the gigantic family wedding set for the tail end of my time off. All those seeds that started dropping in were tiny little gifts.

It made waiting for the breakdown to begin something that I was excited about! I had no idea when the idea of a breakdown surfaced that this would be the case. But I am so grateful that it is.

Oh — and an extra-big thank-You for knowing that I needed to mask my pending breakdown as a sabbatical. That was so clever. Once I did that, I could talk openly with my friends and family about my plans. They had no idea that the impetus for this supposedly amazing four-week sabbatical was a breakdown on the floor of my closet and the realization that I needed time to correct course on my seemingly perfect life that was anything but. They will find out in time and so will I.

Always,
Me

In the months leading to my breakdown, I marveled at the tiny yet magical ways that space began to seep into my life and slowly reveal in small subtle ways that life could be different. There were also gigantic thuds in the form of people that started to appear. Through a variety of serendipitous circumstances, psychics, astrologers, mediums, mystics, chakra healers, a pastor, his wife, and new friends started to descend into my world in random, unexpected, and alluring ways. I did not seek out this cast of characters. Rather than immediately dismiss them as simply mildly intriguing or a form of entertainment, a new sense of curiosity and exploration opened within that allowed me to consider without judgment all they brought into my life.

I had visited psychics at various points. It was typically from a place of part boredom, part mild intrigue mixed in with a twist of *what the hell*. It certainly was not from any deep belief system that these people could accurately tell me my future. I was too logical to ever allow myself to believe that. I was just curious, mildly fascinated yet highly skeptical.

Growing up, my family and I visited India several times. On each trip, I insisted that my aunt take me to the neighborhood astrologer. She would always oblige. It was a quick, five-minute walk to the astrologer's home. In India, they have astrologers the way we have neighborhood 7-Elevens. We were seated on the floor while we waited for the astrologer to arrive. The small room was filled floor-to-ceiling with tattered astrology books, pictures of deities on the walls, and incense wafted in the air. My aunt gave the astrologer the date, time, and city of my birth. The astrologer then carefully selected a book and began flipping through it until he landed on the magical page that told him my future. I would lean in to hear what he said. He spoke fast and in an Indian dialect that was hard for me to follow. The astrologer talked about one planet being more prominent in my chart than another. He rattled on quickly about the impact of these planetary positions on my future — mostly marriage, career, and family.

My aunt listened intently and peppered the astrologer with more specific questions on the timing of when I would meet my future mate and whether this man would be any good for me. The astrologer answered with confidence on his predictions based on the stars. He even offered recipes to improve my fate: donating black blankets to an orphanage or feeding orange fish in a free-flowing pond (yes, really). Other remedies included going into a park with a small mirror, hugging a tree and watching myself do it while I threw rice over one shoulder. The details were always complicated, and I was never sure I did it quite right. Once my aunt was satisfied with the answers and the proposed remedies, we needed to make my future husband come sooner, be taller and more handsome (yes, I am serious), we paid the astrologers and were on our way.

Some of it resonated. Some seemed improbable. As riveting as the experience was, I took it all as entertainment and not as anything serious that would make me alter the progression of my life. I was firmly rooted in logic. Astrologers, palm readers and the like weren't going to change that, as enticing as it all was. As my aunt and I would walk away from the astrologer's tiny abode, we would dissect what he said and laugh. We would extrapolate more meaning from his simple words than perhaps he intended. My aunt always concluded our astrological adventures with the same phrase. *"We in India have these astrologers and you in America have therapists. It's just what people need to help themselves feel better."*

Yet during the period leading to my breakdown, something felt different. Instead of being just a temporary pick-me-up, these interactions felt deeper. There was something about each conversation that resonated well beyond my thinking mind. There was a distinct sensation that their words warranted more than just a passing thought. They needed my consideration. Unlike prior jaunts, I couldn't immediately dismiss these people or what they said. I couldn't immediately jump back to my more logical self within minutes of leaving their presence. Something hung in the air and stayed with me. I started to recognize that they weren't giving me a magic recipe to transform life. What they were doing was giving me tiny hints in the right direction that unlocked one door after another until I was equipped enough to unlock them for myself. Instead of the drifting feather or being stopped in my tracks by a cute puppy, these were Soul Sparks in human form and they were dropping like big, giant flares.

Take Diane. Diane was a psychic with a PhD, a strong Southern accent and ended almost every sentence with *"that's what I am talking about."* She was scattered, unorganized, but she spoke to my spirit and her insights were riveting. Normally I can't handle being around people on the opposite end of the spectrum from me, but with her none of that mattered. When she spoke, she shook my soul. She could see parts of myself that I could not see or was unwilling to acknowledge. She saw beneath the armor and within seconds illuminated with perfect accuracy the challenges of my life. She knew facts and circumstances that were deeply private and not spoken to a soul. She knew that I needed to make big changes to go where I was meant to be.

Over the next several months, we spoke many times and each time she added another nugget that perfectly resonated. I wanted to believe all she said, but my logical self would jump back in and make me question why I spoke with her in the first place and why I kept speaking with her. Yet when life felt terribly off course and desperation kicked in, I couldn't help but wonder if what she was saying was true. Could my life change in the dramatic ways that she predicted?

During one of our conversations, I told her that I couldn't see the path from the life I lived to what she was predicting. She then said something that put my thinking mind in a tizzy but reverberated deeply with my developing spiritual senses. She said, *"Honey, it don't matter if you can't see it. The Universe is pushing this rock up the hill and it's 'bout to come down the other side and ain't nothing you gonna be able to do about it!"* She was right once again.

Even more intriguing were the serendipitous ways these characters began popping up in my life. The charming and charismatic lady who shaped my eyebrows casually mentioned a non-denominational prayer service she and her husband held on Friday evenings. In the five years that I had been going to her, she never mentioned that her husband was a pastor, that they had a church — and she certainly never invited me before. But that day, as she threaded away, she described the service as a place where friends, family and church members gathered to decompress from the week, share their stories of gratitude or angst, engage in non-denominational prayer, enjoy a potluck, and then do karaoke. I had no idea what the karaoke had to do with anything, but I was intrigued enough to want to check it out. I asked my friend to join me. Little did I know that one visit would be the beginning of a long and lovely relationship between me, the pastor, and his wife.

It was a welcoming and inviting place, albeit a little rundown and dated. Paint peeled from the walls. The heat never worked quite right no matter how many times someone went to check the thermostat. The faded green carpet had certainly seen better days. But none of that mattered once you settled in. This place was magic. There were typically between 10 and 15 people. We all sat in a circle in the church's multipurpose room. The Pastor warmly welcomed each of us individually as we walked in. He was a jovial and warmhearted man in his early 50s with bright eyes and an engaging smile. With his simple welcome he made me feel that I belonged. His wife gave me the same warm inviting hug and smile she did when I walked into her salon. She always made me feel like we were the best of friends. *"Hello, my dear sweet Deepika,"* she would say so warmly her eyes twinkling with wonderment and love. *"I made delicious chai for you this evening. Come let me pour you a cup."* Her tea was one of the many highlights. The aroma of ginger, cardamom and cinnamon in her special chai made my nose tingle with delight.

The pastor would begin each session by inviting everyone to let go of their week, to shake off the bad and to be grateful for the good. He asked each person to share something with the group. One by one, person by person, we shared. An ailment. A work conflict. A simple and happy moment with a child. The Pastor would offer his thoughts about the week and how it connected to the Divine. Last, we would pray. Without reference to any particular god or belief system, we would pray. We would pray for ourselves, for each other and the world around us. It was there that I first learned how beautifully meditation and prayer seamlessly blended together.

Every week was different. The church was a place to come together to set new intentions. It was a place to express gratitude, so much gratitude, for all life had given everyone in attendance. It was also a place to share pain, heartbreak, and sorrow. It was a place to hear other people's stories about how the Universe was quite literally showing them the way, one small step at a time. It was also fun. There were laughter, jokes — and don't forget the karaoke! These folks would belt out pop tunes once the main gathering was over.

These prayer gatherings were yet another shift. I was letting myself say no to all that was not adding to my life (such as meaningless dinner parties where the talk was all about who was doing what with whom and when) and in so doing I created space to attend these Friday night gatherings. I engaged with a community of people experiencing life — good, bad, and the in-between — and where remaining grounded in faith, gratitude and a strongly-held belief that the Divine had a great plan for each of them. Even if at that moment in their sorrow, angst, struggle, or fatigue they could not see it, they believed it. Slowly, I did, too.

I attended that Friday night service every week for about a year. I masked my attendance to my husband as a yoga class. I didn't want anyone's ridicule or judgment and he would surely do both if he knew I was attending a church. While he and I were of different religions, he a Hindu and I a Sikh, he wouldn't be able to understand why I would choose to go to church and I certainly didn't feel like explaining it, especially to him. He would not be able to understand that this was less about a specific religion and more about the elements of shared belief systems. It was a transformative experience that spoke to me in ways I was unable to fully understand and appreciate at the time.

Serendipitous moments led to major steps. I will never forget one such interaction. It was my friend's 40th birthday and she hosted a wine-tasting party at a small family winery perched up on a hill overlooking the bay. The day of the party was cold and the party was outdoors, so I was bundled up in a warm jacket. All the guests were huddled up close together near the outdoor heaters as we sipped the lovely wines, shared sweet treats, and toasted our dear friend.

There was a woman who I had never met before in attendance. She was short with bouffant hair. She was a bit reserved yet engaged in the conversations that were springing up. Every now and again she would walk away from the group to stand alone. It happened multiple times. She would be with the group, engaged, laughing and then walk about 20 feet away where she would stand alone for about five minutes before walking back to the group.

I was drawn to her. I needed to connect with her. I told myself that the next time she walked away from the group I would approach her. As the party was near an end, I finally mustered up enough courage to walk up to her. I said, quite directly and in a manner that I haven't done before, *"I find you so interesting and I am drawn to your energy."* I was surprised that these words even came out of my mouth. I am not sure I have ever said *"I am drawn to your energy"* to anyone. EVER. It would have sounded ridiculous to most people but to her it resonated completely.

People have said this exact phrase to me before. In fact, it happened twice: once while walking down a busy San Francisco street and the second time in a crowded mall. When it happened, I was taken so off guard that my only reaction was to walk a little faster and not meet their gaze. I didn't think these people were crazy, but I didn't know what would happen after that sentence and, back then, I wasn't keen to find out. This time was different. I was the one saying the energy line — and, in that moment, it was completely authentic. Fortunately, it was also well received. The young woman looked at me and smiled. She said *"I am feeling someone's energy very heavily right now. Maybe it is you."* I felt an immediate Soul Spark and responded, *"Maybe it is."*

Turns out this woman, in addition to being a physical therapist, was a psychic who did chakra healings. Within a few minutes of standing together in the vineyard, she just looked at me and said, *"You are going to be okay."* I am not sure why those words came from her mouth at that moment, but they resonated so deeply.

On the drive to the party I was overcome with emotion, distressed, saddened, and bewildered by my life and the circumstances I was finding myself in. My husband and I had gotten into yet another argument. I left for the party defeated and depleted. Despite the shifts and clear messages from the Universe appearing in my life, I was still questioning my beliefs and questioning how and when things would get better. Her intuition picked up on all of that, which is why her words felt like a divine reminder, or Soul Spark, to stay the course.

We started meeting regularly in her tiny yet inviting healing studio. During our sessions, as she spoke I could see her physically connect with the Divine to deliver the messages I needed to hear. She would tilt her head towards the sky, her eyes would shift upward and flutter like butterfly wings. I would follow her gaze to see if I could physically see whatever she was connecting with, but I would just find myself staring at the light fixtures or the color of the paint on the ceiling.

Through our conversations, she helped me to understand more fully how our lives are constantly speaking to us and that we just need to be open to receiving the messages. Through her guidance, I learned techniques, some related to chakras and some just related to life, that helped me be more open to the ways of the Universe. It was yet another way that just by creating tiny spaces within myself to receive, I could hear a message about where I was in my life and where I needed to head.

The Universe presented these people at these exact moments in my life to propel me forward on my spiritual journey. It knew I wasn't going to go willingly where I needed to go. Logic was going to impede any possible leaps of faith that I needed to make. By creating some space and openness, however slight, I had room to let people in. And boy, did they start showing up. Person after person began to descend into my life to help take me one step forward, however slowly, to the person I needed to become. I needed them to open the doors, help me see my life circumstances in a new light, because left to my own logic-driven devices, I wasn't going to get there.

When I visited astrologers, psychics, mediums, or even prayed deeply in church, I was just going outside of myself for answers that I was fully capable of unlocking from within myself. I just didn't know how to tune into my own truths. The gateway to turning more fully inward for me was coming across so many people, one after another, as if the Universe had lined them all up. As if I was meant to bump into each one of them in rapid succession while waiting for my breakdown. As if each one was meant to help me, little by little, not only hear what my innermost self was saying but also to believe in it, too. Through these conversations, I learned that spirituality was attainable and accessible to me. I didn't need a shaman, a guru, or even a yoga instructor to unlock it for me. With time I was able to unlock it for myself.

Hello Friend,

If you told me before my breakdown that I would meet a cast of characters who would serve as conduits for my greater understanding of the Universe, I probably would have laughed. Scratch that. I DEFINITELY would have laughed. When you operate with logic and facts, you can't imagine that seemingly random people will keep showing up in your life and shake things up in ways that you can't imagine. Yet for me, that is exactly what happened. Person after person kept entering my world, dropping messages from the Universe that changed my life in the best possible ways.

Likely, this has happened in your life too.

Try This

Scroll through the contacts in your phone and look at each person's name. How many of these people showed up in your life randomly but ended up playing a much bigger role? Go through each person and think about how they first came into your life. Then reflect on the role they have in your life now. There will be some who started as, and remained, simply acquaintances. But there are likely others that have impacted your life in ways you could not have anticipated when you first met.

Give it a try.

Always,
Me

HELLO UNIVERSE, IT'S ME

CHAPTER 5

Hello Universe,

It is finally here and I couldn't be more excited. Five months ago, I was crying in my closet desperate for a break but literally had no time to take one. Now all that waiting is over. Breakdown time is here. I am strangely excited. I mean who feels like dancing when a breakdown is coming? But here I am! I waited five long months to even begin the process of figuring out what to fix and how. It is here now and couldn't be more thrilled.

Fortunately, You presented some pretty great shifts, albeit small ones, to get me through these five months. You also presented some interesting people — so many of them — that I really do believe were messengers You orchestrated to pop into my life to keep the shifts happening. You do work in mysterious ways. Good thing I am on to You now.

You also presented a fair share of heartbreaks, disappointments, and continuing frustrations while I was waiting for the breakdown to begin. Instead of these incidents making way to another cry session in my closet or something worse, they instead were just added to the ever-growing list of what needed processing during my time off.

Well, I made it. The time is now. Let's see what this breakdown has in store.

Always.
Me

I am one of those women who had to mask time for myself as something other than what it was. When I would go for a short walk around the block it was to get enough privacy to talk openly and candidly to my sister about my marriage. Sometimes, I would tell my husband that I was going to run errands and then get groceries but really, I was taking an hour to get a much-needed massage. Other times, I would fake a work trip to Los Angeles — but really, I longed to sip champagne poolside at my mom's house for some overdue uninterrupted rest, relaxation, and motherly love. I couldn't even call my breakdown a breakdown. I couldn't have it when I needed to have it most. I had to wait until I could schedule it in and disguise it as a well-deserved sabbatical.

Getting to this point was exhausting. To be away from work for a month was no small feat. It required detailed planning so that in my absence my projects would keep running smoothly. Unlike most professionals these days, my intention was to be fully disconnected from the office. That meant no more buzzing phone every time an email came through. No more obsessively checking for the latest client crisis that needed my attention. I went so far as to not just disable notifications of new emails from my phone; I deleted the mail app all together. For us whose phones are just another limb at the end of our hands, this is not easy or comfortable (it was pretty much terrifying) but I had an overwhelming sensation that if I was to make bigger shifts, then I needed to sideline any unnecessary distractions. I needed to be fully present in my breakdown to let the shifts, changes and movements forward take hold. Checking in on work, even if it was just a glance at my email or taking one work call here and there, as I normally would when on vacation, would be a life vest to leave my breakdown and go back to being the person with whom I was most familiar. I did not want to do that.

I decided to give myself a lot of structure to *be* unstructured. Each day went something like this:

8:30 - Drop daughter at preschool

9:00 - Yoga

10:30 - Journaling at coffee shop

12:30 - Pick up daughter from preschool

2:00 - Painting

5:00 - Prep dinner and evening routine with daughter

7:00 - More journaling, reading and meditating

This was such a stark contrast from my normal workday schedule, where every meeting was back-to-back. Driving to see a client was never just a drive. It was filled with a conference call and, depending on the length of the drive, sometimes more than one. I was rushing, always leaving one meeting a few minutes early to get to the next one a few minutes late. To have free time during the day and open spaces would be an absolute luxury.

The breakdown schedule also focused on creativity. I always loved to write. I kept a journal off and on (mostly on) from the age of 12. I wrote for my high school and college newspapers. I did an internship with the *San Diego Union-Tribune*. I started and stopped various writing projects through the years from a wedding blog to a book about my online-dating adventures. If my time off had lots of open spaces, I was sure to rekindle my writing passion and put down on paper whatever needed to come out of me. I didn't have any idea what that would be, but I figured with time, a pen in hand and a beautiful journal gifted to me by a friend, I would surely figure it out.

I also wanted to paint. I caught the bug at a work team-building event. It was one of those trendy wine-and-paint parties. It was held in what appeared from the outside to be a standard, non-descript, slightly underloved 1970's office building. I walked in, climbed the steps to the second floor and roamed the halls tentatively to find the right spot. Then there it was, tucked away in a corner, Suite 202. As I opened the door, I was mesmerized. The office space was transformed into a Parisian street, complete with a beret-wearing paint teacher and French music streaming from the speakers. I was greeted with a lovely glass of sparkling wine and warmly directed to a spot in the class where a medium-sized white canvas, paints, and paintbrushes greeted me.

The minute I took the brush in my hand it felt like a natural extension of myself. I was mesmerized by the gorgeous colors laid out before me. The canvas, blank and white, was just waiting for my creativity to fill each inch with whatever I deemed fit. I was hooked.

My breakdown presented a perfect opportunity to get deeper into painting. Through a friend of a friend, I happened upon Tina. She was in her late 40's. She spent her life raising her two kids and painting in her garage whenever she could spare the time. Now that her kids were in high school and college, they needed her far less. She could now not only paint for her own pleasure, but she could also return to her first passion — teaching. She taught painting to groups of kids and adults, like me.

We started painting together several times a week from her home studio. Her gentle mannerisms, painting knowledge, and loving patience as I learned were nothing short of a blessing. We painted mostly flowers of various shapes, sizes, and depths. Within seconds of beginning each session, I became immersed as I perfected each flower petal on my canvas. Sometimes two hours would pass in what felt like seconds as I blended shades of pink and green to near-perfection (let me tell you, there are more shades than you can imagine). I slowly became acquainted with the various brushes and the opportunities each presented to create a petal that was as realistic as possible.

It was mindfulness in the truest sense of the word. Not only was I fully present with each stroke on my canvas, I also learned to be more aware of my surroundings. Before these classes, I never fully considered the shape of a flower, the various colors on a single petal, or even the angles that Mother Nature presents so effortlessly on everything from a blade of grass to a tree trunk. I realized the depth of our world not just as a whole but in each speck that makes up even the tiniest of spaces. The experience made me step back and take notice of every cloud, the curve of each hill, the way the light hits buildings just so. I learned so much painting with her.

No one is more surprised than me that I was able to be this present, this aware, this Zen during my scheduled breakdown. Before my time off, if you had said to go get lost in a painting, my response would have been: *"Huh?"* Yet during my time off, the simple fact that I gave myself permission to go deeper within myself, that I removed many of the day-to-day blockers that create so much unnecessary noise and distraction meant that I was able to be present and thoroughly immersed in something as lovely as painting strokes of a flower petal.

Giving my creativity an outlet was an important part of my sabbatical. Another important part was yoga and meditation. Lots of it. I had been practicing yoga off and on for 15 years. It was a calming, centering and invigorating practice that opened me up in important ways. I knew that having wide-open days meant I could go to yoga almost daily with the stay-at-home moms and retirees in my community. I figured only good could come from doing more yoga. By opening myself up (quite literally) realizations would certainly flow.

But it was meditation that surprisingly and unexpectedly became the star of my time off. I didn't know that I would so deeply connect with meditation during this time or that I would do it with such regularity. It certainly wasn't part of the plan. Yet at my local yoga studio, the instructor would start and end of each yoga class with a guided meditation. In her beautiful and gentle voice she would say, *"Close the eyes and take a deep intentional breath. In through the nose and out through the mouth."* She would say to clear the mind of the days to-do lists, of the troubles, of the worries. She would guide us to stay with the breath and leave all our thoughts behind.

As a newbie to meditation, my mind was rarely if ever free of thoughts. Being on my breakdown did not mean that all my troubles vanished. There was plenty of commotion. I still had a kid who didn't sleep well. A house that needed to be cared for. And a husband who was just being him on steroids — more irritable, more disengaged, more disparaging. But during these moments with her, in this class, with other students, all breathing intentionally and trying to let go of the day-to-day stresses, trying to be fully present in the breath, something magical happened. I longed to be in that moment longer and longer.

I started to devour everything I could about meditation and how to teach myself to meditate more consistently and ultimately more deeply. I found an app for my phone that did exactly that. I cozied up in my favorite spot, put on my headphones, tapped the app, and heard a beautiful soothing voice, just like my yoga teacher's, guiding me through the meditation. Her voice alone eased so much of my day's tension.

The meditation teacher on my phone always began with *"clear your mind."* Clearing your mind is no easy feat when your mind is as cluttered and busy as mine. Seriously, my mind was equivalent to a crowded subway station in the middle of New York City. There were mobs of people, talking, screaming, listening to music, laughing, checking their cell phones all packed in like sardines waiting for their train to arrive so they could hurriedly go wherever it is they were going.

I started by visualizing myself above that crowded subway platform, watching the people packed shoulder-to-shoulder waiting for their train to arrive. I would carefully select one noisy person at a time, tap them on the shoulder, gently pluck them by the collar, and pull them out of the scene. Then another. Then another. There was no method to who I pulled out or in what order. I just slowly started to move them out one by one. I would thank them for being here in my messy subway-station brain and ask them to kindly move out of the way. In so doing, I began to not just create space in my fictitious subway station, but also in my mind. As the crowd began to lift, there was finally space and that space was glorious. That feeling was expansive. That feeling was comforting. That feeling was freedom. That feeling was oozing with clarity. I would dial up this sensation during my meditation.

I would sit with myself in that space for as long as I could. It started slowly, five minutes here and 10 minutes there. But eventually I was regularly able to do 20-to-30-minute meditations. I no longer needed the app and could easily guide myself into this space. I learned to not just be quiet and slow down my thoughts but to also allow myself the space and the time for whatever was within me to bubble up to the surface. Not the list of what chores needed to get done or what items I needed from the grocery store on my way home or the people I needed to email. But to really hear all that was buried deep within me that needed to come to the surface.

Best of all, meditation and the way I structured my days gave me time to be fully present with my daughter. From the moment she was born and the nurses handed her into my arms, I knew she and I had been together through many lifetimes. It was not the first time we saw each other. As I examined her tiny feet, her perfect little hands, and her big brown eyes, I knew our souls were mostly certainly connected beyond this current earthly realm. Which isn't to say, that we are similar. She is spunky, energetic, courageous, and brave beyond measure. She is a daredevil through and through. Me? I am the complete opposite. Always tentative, extremely cautious, more reserved, and not at all willing to go down a zip line or a sit in the front row of a scary rollercoaster. Yet, I am learning to not let my own limitations or upbringing shape the way I parent her. I am learning to be more open and willing to engage in her adventures and indulge her curiosities, as scary as they may seem to me.

Being with her and being her mom is my life's greatest gift and it is the reason that this staycation breakdown was the best choice for me. I didn't want to leave her behind while I was finding myself. I wanted to find myself with her right there by my side. So instead of trying to get away, I wanted to be as fully present in my day-to-day life to understand, contemplate, reflect, and change. Even day-to-day annoyances of life — like being woken up way by the loud garbage truck, stubbing my toe as I got out of bed, or even a pile of dishes in the sink — no longer impacted the calmness of my day.

It took a few days to ease into doing far less than I normally did but slowly the changes took hold. Daily painting, yoga, journaling, and meditation let my mind quiet and wind down from the stresses that built up inside of me. Slowly, the pressures eased and gave way to new understandings. Even the day-to-day activities I had to do — like doing the laundry or taking out the trash — became acts of mindfulness that I learned to enjoy and embrace with a different vantage point. I took satisfaction from being productively unproductive and loved the challenge of finding a slower rhythm to life. What was not slow, was the number of epiphanies that came forward during this time. Life was speaking to me and thankfully, I was listening.

Hello Friend,

Right here, right now, I am giving you permission to do you. I am giving you whatever hug, confident look in the eye, or Soul Spark you need to go do what you need to do to keep your life on track. If you are desperate for a break, if you need to reset your life and you need to take time for yourself but don't know if you can or should do it, I am here to say loudly and with love — you can do it, friend. You should do it. And you must do it.

The way you take time to reexamine and look at your life may be different. You may feel the need to run off for a vacation. You may feel like I did, and just want to re-do you in your own daily environment. Or you may have some other longing that you wish to explore. Whatever it is, I give you permission to set out and do it.

Some of you may have no clue where to start or how to reset. That's okay too. By slowly quieting the mind and setting an intention, you can find your way. Here is a mantra that I used often in the months leading up to my breakdown. I offer it to you here to see if it may resonate with you.

"Right now, in this moment I rejoice in allowing myself nurturing, calming and complete acceptance of who I am. My ability to fill up my reservoir in this manner invites vibrance, creativity and moves me forward to the next dimension of my life's purpose."

You may wish to recite this mantra out loud. You may repeat it to yourself several times. You may prefer to write it down in a journal or on a beautiful piece of paper. You may type it out, print it and keep it with you so you can revisit it as you traverse your path. However you choose to use this mantra, I hope it embraces your being and gives you solace.

Always,
Me

HELLO UNIVERSE, IT'S ME

CHAPTER 6

Hello Universe,

I didn't know how hard it would be to do nothing. I felt anxious that I wasn't sending 100 emails a day. I felt anxious that I wasn't attending every client meeting. It even felt weird to no longer run out of the house in a rush every morning. It was as if I was cheating by going to yoga in the middle of the day or sipping a latte while daydreaming at the coffee shop for hours. I get that some people's careers allowed them this luxury but mine surely did not.

Thankfully, that angst slowly dissipated. The open space let my brain decompress and see past all the noise and distractions. All that commotion was just a security blanket to avoid the deeper feelings and emotions that I actively pushed aside for years.

You were well aware that this is what would happen to me during this time off, weren't you? You knew that at first I would want to jump right back into my regular, busy life. That I would gravitate towards what was familiar to me. That I would be tempted to give up. That I would want to shift back to productivity as my shield for avoiding the breakdown and experiencing all I needed to experience.

Fortunately, I didn't give up on me. I did enough of that in my life. No more. I was ready to show up for me. Whenever the doubt crept in, You just kept showing me the way to stay where I needed to be to get to where I was meant to be.

This time off was a perfectly curated gift from You. You made sure that during this time I would have a healthy dose of laughter and fun just to keep things balanced. You can't be hyper-introspective all the time. I mean, it's good to go within, but sometimes you need to laugh it all out with your girlfriends. That is exactly what happened during my time off — laughter, fun and some deep revelations courtesy of my best friend, Mindi.

Keep showing me the way.

Always,
Me

The wide-open spaces of the sabbatical blended together perfectly with a few small trips over the weekends when my husband could easily look after our daughter. It was a rarity that I ever left my daughter and went away. Since she was born, I had probably left her twice with just her Dad — once for a two-day business trip to New York and once for a night in Southern California with my sister a few months before her wedding. Going away without my daughter was a rare gift of solo time — and during this month it was going to happen twice. The weekend trips offered the perfect mix of doing nothing and deep reflection balanced with fun, laughter, and exuberance. Little did I know every portion of this carefully contrived breakdown would bring giant gongs from the Universe that could not be ignored no matter how hard I tried.

Two of my best friends, my sister, and I ventured off to Vancouver for a weekend to celebrate my 40th. Food tours, spas, lounges, shopping, lots of walking and laughing made it a spectacular trip. We even spent time with my childhood best friend who lived in Vancouver. We got dressed up. We enjoyed live music. We talked. We connected and had the best of times.

On the last day of the trip at the airport, each friend left one by one to a different gate to take their flight: one back to Seattle, the other back to Los Angeles. Big hugs were had for each gal pal as we parted and we made the obligatory closing statement that we would for sure do it all again soon. Mindi and I had later flights to San Francisco which let us enjoy a glass of wine together in the airport bar before departing. We'd been friends since our junior year of college. Of the bunch of us that hung out during college, it was most unlikely that she and I would remain the closest of friends. She was a tiny, spunky, quirky, smart Polish girl from Indiana. I was a stylish, trendy, pop-culture-obsessed Indian girl from Los Angeles. Yet, we shared the most beautiful friendship. Through breakups, heartaches, the deaths of our dads and so much more, we went through it all together.

As we sipped wine to the background noise of airport announcements of arriving and departing flights, Mindi asked, *"What are you learning from all this time off?"* I sighed one of those big sighs. The one that makes a sound a little too loudly. She was my truest of true friends. I knew I could not hide what I felt in that moment. I also knew that whatever I shared would stay in the strictest confidence. Tears formed as I looked at her. I said, *"I dread being in my house when my husband is home."*

It wasn't a new feeling. It was a sensation that I long experienced but successfully avoided acknowledging. Even uttering these words now to my best friend gave the sensation of fear and relief. Fear of not knowing the implication of this realization. But now with all my time off, it was not a feeling I could bury away any longer. When I was with my friends, with my daughter, or with my family, I was the most real, most authentic version of me. In those moments, I felt like my truest self. But when I found myself around my husband, I felt forced to be someone I was not. I masked and minimized my professional successes for fear he would feel threatened or that he would belittle my accomplishments. Perhaps it was unintentional. Perhaps it made him feel better about himself. I don't really know. What I do know is that I was constantly pumping him up to make sure he felt good in his life no matter how it made me feel about my own.

I came to realize that, somewhat subconsciously, I transitioned into my wife costume when I got home from work. Sort of like when Clark Kent would leave his newspaper job and rip off his shirt and tie to reveal his Superman suit. I would leave the version of my normal, everyday self on the curb outside my house like a trash pile. But instead of a superhero costume underneath my work attire, I had a pair of yoga pants and a hoodie. Instead of transforming into something great like a superhero ready to save the day, I would just leave my enthusiasm, my go-getterness, my ambition, my zest outside next to my garbage cans so I could retrieve it the next time I left the house. In my wife costume, I didn't share much about my day. I didn't share the successes I was enjoying. Instead, I tiptoed around my husband to make sure I didn't say anything that would offend him. I worked instead to pump him up so he felt like he was enough, that he was worthy. That whatever he did at his job or in his day was the best to have ever happened.

I don't remember quite when this started. Maybe it was the time a colleague at work nominated me for the Silicon Valley of Women of Influence award through the local business journal. This was an honor bestowed upon 50 women each year in the areas of business, technology, government, not-for-profit, and healthcare sectors. Not only was I nominated — but I was selected for the award. The newspaper planned to celebrate the winners at a large banquet. I was so proud, excited, stunned to be nominated but to also be selected for this honor. It felt incredible. I called my mom first. She beamed with pride the way she always did whenever one of my siblings or I achieved something great. *"Wow — Beeki!"* That was her nickname for me after the character Beeker in the Muppets since I mumbled a lot when I was little, Beeker's key trait. *"See you are working so hard and now people are recognizing you for it. This is so exciting!"*

Later that day, when I got home, I told my husband. I thought for sure he would beam with pride for me too. *"Oh, that's nice"* he said. *"But they gave it to a lot of people. It's not that big a deal. It's not like you are getting an award alongside some big wig like Marissa Mayer or Carly Fiorina. They are the women who really influence Silicon Valley. But yeah, good work."* Yes, I was not the CEO of Yahoo or Hewlett Packard. And yes, the two of them were not getting this award, but I was and it was a tremendous honor for me. Sure, I am not influencing Silicon Valley boardrooms the way the two of them might be, but I was doing something right as this organization was about to honor me for my accomplishments.

Mindi reminded me in the loving and kind way that she always presented her observations without judgment: *"In all the years you have been with him, you regularly made excuses for his behaviors and the way he made you feel."* She was right. The problem was that it had gone on for so long and had become the rhythm of the relationship for me to pump him up and force myself to be small around him to keep our home life stable. For someone who has such a zest for life, who is such a go-getter, who wants to do more and be better at everything I tackle, acting small in this way was a betrayal of my truest self. Yet I did it. Time after time. Month after month. Day after day. I did it. I took solace in friends, especially Mindi, when it came to the disappointment I felt in my marriage — yet I chose to remain disappointed. Perhaps he was indifferent. Perhaps he was unaware. Perhaps he simply didn't care. Perhaps it was his power move. To this day, I don't know what his experience within our marriage was. All I know is that I had a costume on at all times around him. I couldn't be my truest self.

My friend patiently listened to the thoughts that were surfacing as a result of my open time to think, write, paint and contemplate the circumstances of my life, particularly my marriage, more freely. She heard me complain before. We had been friends for 20 years. She knew every boyfriend, every heartache, every struggle, every success. She saw me overflowing with joy and broken with sadness. She knew all too well the angst I experienced with my husband back when he was my boyfriend and throughout the marriage. She also saw how hard I worked to keep the marriage moving. She knew how many times I had suggested marital counseling and how my husband always refused. How he could be better for a few months at a time, then revert to old behaviors, and how sad that made me.

She listened patiently this time, as always. Then, right there in the airport lounge, she made the most crystalizing observation that stayed with me throughout my breakdown and became the lens with which I viewed my relationship with my husband from that moment onwards: *"In all the time I have known you with him, you have vacillated between disliking him and tolerating him. Never have you expressed true love or happiness with him or your relationship.*" I had never considered our relationship in those terms, but she expressed so perfectly what had been bubbling up inside of me for so long.

It was then that I realized I didn't want to wake up at 50 and complain about the same things that I was complaining about a decade earlier. Something needed to change. I just didn't know what or how.

Hello Friend,

We have all experienced a moment where we realize something needs to change. The problem is we don't always act on it. Maybe that is okay. Maybe every problem doesn't need to be solved. Maybe every closed door doesn't need to be re-opened. I don't know. But what I do know is that we sometimes keep doing the same things, in the same way, because it is familiar to us, not because it is good for us. We stay in the same patterns; we tolerate the same behaviors because it is comfortable for us. We know what it feels like to be in the situations that we are in. It's familiar. Just because tolerating certain behavior is familiar to us, and we know how to do it, doesn't mean it should continue.

Sometimes we don't know that we deserve better. I am here to tell you, clearly and with love that you do deserve better. If you have been dealing with a situation that is draining you, that makes you sad, frustrates you, or just makes you mad, continuing to tolerate something that you know isn't good for you, I want you to know that you can break free. You can create a new normal for yourself that isn't draining, that isn't toxic, that isn't breaking you. You can create the changes you need for you to live your best life. You can do it. All the forces of the Universe are conspiring to take you there. You just need to be clear on what you want and be willing to put in the work.

 Take a moment to settle into the feeling you have on the days when everything feels aligned. For some, these days may rarely exist. For others they may not be days, but moments. Whatever it is for you, I want you to be *fully in that space. Be in the days when you wake up in the morning, your house is nice and quiet, there is no chore on the to-do list. There is no mad dash to get somewhere fast. It's the day where you get to spend every minute doing something you love, something that inspires you, something that excites you. Every interaction or occurrence in your day is one where you feel fully supported and aligned because you are doing that which you enjoy most.*

In these moments, how do you feel? What sensation do you notice as you traverse these days? Write down the thoughts that come to you. It can be a list of words, feelings, or you can write out the experience in greater detail. Really feel into the sensation that these types of days bring you. Now, I want you to imagine waking up to a life where this is how you felt every day. How would that be?

Once you are done, I want you to acknowledge that you already know how to feel this way. All you need to uncover is the time in each day to do something that cultivates these feelings for you. It may feel daunting at first, but over time it will happen with ease. By carving out some small parcels of time in each day, you will begin to feel more aligned, connected, and uplifted.

Always,
Me

HELLO UNIVERSE, IT'S ME

CHAPTER 7

Hello Universe,

I am well into my second week of my breakdown and I can confidently say that I am embracing, even loving, this slower pace of life. It took time to unwind into it. When the time off began, it felt a bit unnatural, even a bit forced. Now I am loving this rhythm and I am pretty sure I could stay in this way of life for a lot longer than the four weeks I had planned. But I won't get ahead of myself. I know there is much more to experience during this time off, and I can't wait.

Vancouver was fantastic. Being with Mindi and having some Oprah-style "A-ha moments" was epic. Normally, I would have a realization and jump into action to fix or adjust whatever needed fixing or adjusting. This time, I am going to let that conversation with Mindi simmer. I am sure the rest of my breakdown will shed further light on it. You will make sure of that. There will be action to take at some point but, for now, I just want to ease into the feelings and insights rather than quickly reacting to them.

The silent yoga retreat this week will help. It was always a bucket-list item to go on a yoga vacation. I am not all that sure I can stay silent for four days, but I am willing to try. I have a feeling I will hear lots of messages from You while I am in silence. Bring it.

Always,
Me

The long country road to the Silent Stay Retreat Center in Vacaville was stunning. Farm country on either side of the road. Animals grazing near fences. Beautiful inviting barns and rolling hills. Even though I was less than two hours from home, it felt like I was a thousand miles away. I escaped the hustle-bustle of the Bay Area, the techies, the IPOs, the new millionaires, the inventors, and the investors. I was in farm country now and while the techies used their brains to create cutting-edge technology, I would relax my own to invent my new life. Exiting the freeway and taking this country road for seven miles was a delight. A sensation washed over me. This silent yoga retreat would be exquisite.

I turned right where the farmland gave way to a hill with a steep incline. I drove slowly as my car curved with the hill just twisting and turning going higher and higher until an iron gate with large stone pillars and a simple gold plaque that read "Silent Stay Hermitage" appeared. As the gates opened, the magic began. A long gravel drive gave way to an Italian villa-style estate sitting in the middle of 25 expansive acres. As I parked and entered the property, I was taken by the sheer beauty and simplicity of the place. The views were breathtaking. There were rolling hills in various shades of green and brown for miles in every direction. But more than the scenery, the energy of the hermitage was captivating. The energy hugged you. It almost felt like the sun, the wind, the air, the grass and the trees were all speaking to me and saying, *"You have no idea how much we are going to enjoy our time together."*

I was lucky to find this place. In considering what to do with all my time off, I started to research yoga vacations — something that I always wanted to do but that never previously worked. The timing, the costs, the location.

There was always something that stopped me. Then one lazy rainy Sunday morning while sipping coffee on my couch, I decided to look up one of my favorite yoga teachers from when I first moved to the Bay Area. Back then, Nicole led a Friday night restorative yoga practice that became my happy place. While my cohorts were drinking and partying their Friday nights away, I was regularly at Nicole's Berkeley yoga studio unwinding through long, deeply relaxing poses that let me wear off the week's tension as the sun set outside the studio's floor-to-ceiling windows. I hadn't attended a class with Nicole in more than seven years. But sitting on my couch that morning, I remembered that she led retreats from time to time. I Googled her. Her new yoga studio appeared. There was a link to her retreats for the year. Sure enough, she had one scheduled in the month of June that worked perfectly for me and my budget.

She was there to greet me with a warm hug as I entered the hermitage. It was a big yoga hug. Intentional. Full of love. Showered in blessings. It was a hug full of awareness for all we were about to experience together. In that hug, I felt engulfed not just by her but by the Universe. Through her strong and loving embrace, it felt as if something much larger and bigger than the two of us was embracing. There was strong sense of spiritual knowingness that transcended the two of us in that hug.

Twelve of her students were arriving around the same time. One by one, she gave them the same big warm embrace. I wondered if they felt as I did in that moment. I wondered what their stories were, what brought them there. I wondered what they were doing and thinking as they drove up. Even after four days with each other, I never heard their voices. I never learned their names. I never came to know how their time at the retreat shaped the following days, months, or years of their lives. All I know is that even all these years later, I still see their faces, their gentle and loving smiles and have a feeling of immense gratitude for those 12 people who were part of this journey with me.

The accommodations on the property are best described as a small luxurious dorm room with an attached bath and a balcony. A twin bed with exquisite bedding, a small desk and a cozy chair are all that fit in the room. Yet the tiny space felt more luxurious and liberating than even the fanciest of hotel rooms. Despite the beautiful setting, the lovely accommodations, the amazing yoga teacher who I was seeing after seven years, the kind and gentle faces of my cohorts, once I settled into my room the excitement of being on this retreat gave way to anxiety and fear.

After the first hour at the hermitage, the reality of being in silence for four days started to take hold. I felt as if the walls of the dorm-style room were caving in on me. My heart started racing. My head started to throb. Fear kicked in and I didn't know how to stop it. My mind went into spinning mode.

Can I be silent for four days?

Do I really want to be silent?

This is absurd.

Why am I here?

Shouldn't I be home with my daughter?

Doesn't she need her mom right now?

Why do I want to change my life?

What's wrong with my life anyway?

Am I being selfish?

What will happen in all this silence?

What will I think?

What will I realize?

I am feeling trapped.

I need to leave.

I need to go home.

I need to get out of here.

I don't want to hear whatever this experience is going to tell me.

Get me out of here.

The walls are closing in.

My heart is racing.

What will I do here?

How will I keep myself busy?

Wait, I don't want to be busy.

I wanted to be silent.

I choose this.

I wanted this.

Remember the crying in the closet.

Remember needing to break down.

Remember waiting five months for this moment.

Remember how serendipitous it was to even find this place.

Remember how excited you were on the drive just two hours ago.

Remember this will be good for you.

Remember that warm yoga hug.

Remember feeling like you were meant to be here just a little bit ago.

Spinning and seemingly losing control, I opened the drapes in the small room and stepped out onto the balcony. I released the anxiety one big deep breath at a time. I stepped away from the fears and the questions that started to flood my mind. I reminded myself that I chose this. I wanted to be here. I wanted this month off. I wanted to break down. I wanted to get deep within myself to figure out what I really wanted and needed in my life. Slowly all the deep breaths and fresh air allowed the wave to pass.

The rhythm of the retreat was lovely. I woke up each morning, made a French press coffee in the communal kitchen and then sat on my balcony to be fully present in that moment. I watched the first rays of sun hit the hills. I got lost in the various shades of greens and browns on the mountains. I grew transfixed by the sounds of silence. I smiled as I watched the birds fly by or the little pack of turkeys roam from one end of the property to the other. There were no emails to worry about. No breakfast to make for the family. No conference call to take. Just me, my coffee, the view, the silence.

The retreat schedule was wide open. Our day started at nine in the morning with two hours of meditation and yoga. Then the rest of the day was free to sit in silence, meditate on your own, swim, hike, or just rest. The group reconvened at seven each evening for more yoga and meditation. These bookends to the day left lots of time to think, to observe the amazing surroundings and reflect. I found myself lost in the beautiful blue sky, the picturesque clouds, the hummingbirds, and dragonflies zipping by. It was as if the noisy exteriors of my mind were giving way to layers and layers of peace that lived beneath them. I could simply observe whatever tickled my fancy without a swarm of practical, unnecessary thoughts getting in the way. It was a depth of peace that I had never experienced.

I brought two books along to read and I certainly had ample time to be lost in these books. I also brought my journal. I found so many lovely places to sit — under a tree, on a hammock, at the edge of the pool, on a comfy cozy chair — and just write. The words flowed and flowed. Whatever thoughts, insights or random words came to my mind, I just kept writing them down. Take this passage from the third day of the retreat:

June 16, 2017

I thought this time off might unveil a writing project to pursue or a business venture to launch. But throughout my time off and especially here at Silent Stay, the message coming through is to observe. Observe this current moment. I need to be completely present where I am to see all that is really happening. Observe the leaf falling off the tree. Observe the hummingbird humming along. As, I observe more, I slow down. As I slow down, I am starting to hear the story that my soul wants me to hear. My challenge will be to not just hear what my soul, my spirit, the Universe wants to tell me but to also listen to that message. To honor it and to live it.

I kept writing the word *authentic*. Time and again, it made its way through my fingertips and onto the page. Sometimes, it was just the word. Sometimes it was in the form of a question *(how can I be my most authentic self?)*. Sometimes it was in the context of a mini-epiphany that just appeared seemingly out of nowhere. Day after day, sometimes multiple times a day, that word kept drifting to the surface.

The other thought that kept emerging was a need to slow down. The idea that in order to become my truest, most *authentic* self I needed to keep slowing down. I needed to incorporate activities that allowed myself to release all the tension, the stress, the noise and connected to my inner self. Long hot baths. Walks in nature. Meditation. Watching that hummingbird zip by and really seeing it. The pointed beak, the colors in its wings, and the speed with which it moved. Finding time to pause in my normal everyday life, even if it was only a few minutes at a time, was needed to unlock all the layers of myself and connect more deeply with my inner essence.

There are no coincidences. I was here at this retreat with this yoga teacher at this time because it was completely meant to be this way. And so was everything else. Everything unfolding in my life was part of a larger story. None of it was random. I was being presented with situations, people and even thoughts that were intentionally drifting towards me to transform my life. This realization made me well up with tears. There was a higher power. There was someone or something much bigger than my physical self that was wanting me to see my life in a new way.

Hello Friend,

Have you ever experienced deep peace? Have you ever unwound the brain and all that thinking noise so much that you could hear your soul speak? If you are anything like I was before my scheduled breakdown, the answer is "Nope!" There was never time to unwind deeply. I mean there might have been a good nap here, a nice massage there or a quiet walk in nature. But if it took more than a few hours, I did not afford myself the luxury of ever finding out what that would be like.

Some of you may actively avoid too much silence. Being with oneself for too long can be frightening. You don't know what all that quiet will help you hear. Yet being with ourselves and experiencing that deep silence allows us to get beneath the layers of the day-to-day noise and hear all we are meant to hear.

Try This Imagine yourself sitting in your favorite place where you find solace. For some it may be on the sandy shores of your favorite beach or for others it may be in the mountains amongst the trees or even in the middle of a vibrant urban jungle. Wherever it is that you enjoy for an escape, imagine yourself there. Soften your eyes and allow your mind to take you to this quiet, peaceful space where you feel completely held in nature's embrace. You are uninterrupted. You are safe. You are quiet. As you imagine yourself in this beautiful place, go to the quietest part of yourself, the part of yourself that is open, willing, and able to listen. If you can't find that *place right away, that is okay. Just allow yourself to be in the awareness that you have chosen this time to be with a deeper part of you.*

As you engage in this practice more often, you will start to unleash layers of noise and as you do deeper truths, understandings or insights may emerge. As they do, just jot them down in your journal. Do not judge or attempt to analyze. Just be grateful that in this moment you heard something you have not heard before. Marvel in that.

Always.
Me

HELLO UNIVERSE, IT'S ME

CHAPTER 8

Hello Universe,

Ask and you shall receive. I asked for the privilege of time to break down and reflect and wow, did I get it. Not only have I been able to reflect, I have been able to get to the deepest truths about my own life in a way that I never could before. I was too busy living in a maze that was taking me further and further away from my truest self. Part of me is mad at myself for not being aware of what my life had become and waiting so darn long to make a change. The other part of me is so grateful that I am at least realizing all of this now. And for that, I only have You to thank. I wish I realized this all years ago, but I recognize you only get the revelations when you are ready to receive them. And I am so, so, ready to receive the messages now.

You made sure that I got messages. Some days there were more insights and answers than I felt prepared to receive. Then You decided to go big. Really big. Talk about a Soul Spark. This was a Soul Inferno. There was no turning back now. I heard You loud and clear this time. For that, I thank you.

Always,
Me

Once you strip away the noise, the distractions, the unnecessariness of our days, truths about ourselves, our relationships, our habits become clearer. At some level, we are aware of these truths. We do a masterful job of brushing them off as we double down on the business of life. On another level, while we are aware of these truths, we are terrified to face them.

This made the third week of my sabbatical more intriguing. I had nothing planned for this week, but the Universe sure did. All I intended to do was continue in the usual daily rhythm: dropping my daughter at school, yoga, the coffee shop, journaling and some painting. Oh, and I also planned to see a movie by myself while my daughter was at school (not every moment can be for self-reflection. I needed some fun too!) During this time, one of my husband's friends decided to pay us a visit. He stayed with us a few nights while he attended a relative's wedding nearby. But if you ask me, what he was really here to do was the work of the Universe. He probably never knew it then and I doubt he knows it even now, but the role he played in that week was pivotal. The Universe sent him to push the rock over the hill.

It is my deepest belief that every person comes into our lives for a purpose. There is a method to all the seemingly random madness that occurs in our lives including the cast of characters who appear in them. The grocery-store checkout clerk who gives you a big, loving smile and seems to look deep into your eyes on a day when you are downtrodden and sad. That was not random. The boyfriend who is one of a string who underwhelm and disappoint. He was not random. The teacher who believed in you and gave you the confidence you needed to take the next steps in your life. The teacher was not random.

This is why Dave's arrival was so significant. We had known each other as long as I knew my husband. I don't recall when I first met him or how soon after meeting my husband that took place. He flew into town once or twice a year. We would meet for group vacations or at weddings. We would all hang out together and always had the best time.

Now before your brain jumps too far ahead, there is no story of an illicit affair coming your way. I know you are disappointed, and trust me — I am, too! With all that I eventually had to deal with and answer to, I sort of wish a stormy affair was part of the equation. Not because I wanted anything to transpire with Dave, but because this would make for a much more relatable or predictable story for everyone to digest, including me. Dave's role in my life is much bigger than any romantic twist. He was brought into my life to put in place a series of events that catapulted my life and my spiritual awakening to new heights.

When my husband and I started dating, he was unlike the men I previously went out with. He was the life of every party. He was all about nightclubs, lounges, parties, food, and friends. He was out every Thursday, Friday, and Saturday night exploring new hot spots and riling up his crowd of 20 people to go with him. His evenings would start when I was ready to go to bed. Hanging out at friends' homes or hosting them at his home was a great joy. Simply put, he socialized like it was a competitive sport — and at this he surely took first place.

He won people over with his engaging conversation, his good looks, and his all-around knowledge on every topic. I started calling him Google at one point because there didn't seem to be a topic that he wasn't able to speak about in convincing ways (whether he was right about those topics is another story). He spoke in grandiose terms about what he knew and what he wanted in his life. As our marriage progressed, I realized he was a lot of talk and a lot of inaction. He worked but he didn't have a career. He was filled with excuses for why he didn't advance or why he didn't make more money. He was always in pursuit of a shortcut. A way to get rich quick. He wasn't interested in putting in the work required to do what was needed to get where he wanted to go.

What I also learned over time is that he needed admiration. If he wasn't out doing something that put him front and center, then his personal value diminished. He needed people around to validate him and make him feel important. His own insecurities and lack of confidence made him find external and, in my opinion, artificial sources of validation that gave him a false sense of self.

I was different. I was quiet, not super social, and enjoyed my down time. I was happier being home doing simple things. Even going to the movies on my own was fun for me. Clubs, lounges, bars — none of those places excited me. You are more likely to find me sipping a mimosa poolside with a good book than in a tight, short dress in a loud thumpy club with strobe lights and hundreds of people. If I never go to a loud thumpy music place again, it will be too soon.

We were opposites, and throughout much of our relationship I thought that was okay. He was outgoing. I was more of an introvert. I was career-minded and he was a bit more relaxed about his profession. The one thing I always believed is that my husband had potential. If he could focus and commit to something, anything, he really could be successful. What I didn't know then and discovered during our marriage is that the inner drive to be better, do better, get further that so many of us have on overdrive didn't exist for him and probably never did.

He was a stark contrast to the men I dated before him. My old boyfriends had certain similar traits — polished, sophisticated, successful, hard-working — and some downright brilliant. They were refined, worldly and fun. Their confidence in themselves was backed up with grit, hard work and determination. Take Sam. He was my first true love. Like me, his Dad was a union man and did a hard day's work at the factory in his hometown outside of Detroit. His dad's wish was for his kids to get a great education and to lead better lives than he did. And like me, Sam didn't let his parents down. He was smart beyond measure. Technical and savvy. He went to great schools, finished near the top of his class, got recruited to a great job in Silicon Valley. Through many serendipitous twists he is now a founder and investor in many fast-moving companies.

Most of my exes were like Sam: products of middle-class families who were focused on climbing economic and social ladders the old-fashioned way through a solid education, working hard at their career and advancing. They made it look easy, but they all worked diligently to get to where they were. I had a type.

This is why I always liked Dave. He had all the qualities that I admire — smart, confident, hard-working, self-made. We always got along. We had common interests, experiences, and backgrounds. He was easy to talk to and connect with. I always found him attractive, intelligent, and intriguing. He was impeccably groomed, exceedingly well dressed, he was articulate, well-read, well-traveled, and, despite his vast professional successes, I found him relatable. Did I mention he was handsome? He was very, very, very handsome.

Dave was divorced in his late twenties. I never met his wife. I don't know what happened between them. All I knew is this handsome bachelor was a good catch for my single friends, so I regularly tried to set him up. Those introductions never amounted to much. He never had trouble meeting women, yet he remained mostly single for as long as I knew him. I could never reconcile why such a seemingly good catch was not taken.

I always looked forward to Dave's visits. It meant fun was sure to be had. When a friend like Dave came to town, my husband became the life of the party again. He was happy, engaged, cracking jokes, and just enjoying himself. I enjoyed this version of him more than the overly self-deprecating, self-loathing, insecure, unmotivated man I endured during most of my marriage.

My husband and I were not having much fun. Our marriage was fizzling at a rapid pace, and, really, it was never that good to begin with. My husband knew that my breakdown was born from my need to sort through some type of existential questions. What I don't think he knew then is that some of those questions involved him. Yet as each day of my time off progressed, a distance built between us. As I became more aware of my truths and more in tune with all of the energies around me, I was not only less interested in him but I was also far more aware of how my past behaviors in this relationship landed me right in this spot where I needed to re-examine everything. Spending wide-open spaces in reflection meant starting to see my life from different vantage points. Much of what I was seeing told me something about my relationship with my husband needed to change. I couldn't bear to live in a marriage where in order to survive I had to make myself so incredibly insignificant.

The prospect of someone coming to visit was exciting. It would surely help ease some of the tension in our home, a welcome relief. And so on a Thursday in late June, with my breakdown in full swing, with the new energies swirling in my life, with epiphanies and *a-ha* moments on overdrive, when Dave pulled up to the house, an energetic tsunami pulled up in full force with him. I watched from the window in my daughter's room on the second floor as he arrived. His slow and steady exit from the car. Opening the trunk. Removing his suitcase and garment bag, which undoubtedly included a perfectly pressed and tailored suit he planned to wear to the wedding. He walked up the short drive and then I heard the ring of the doorbell. It was a giant gong from the Universe that nothing was ever going to be the same again.

Within moments I was swept up in his energy. It was overpowering and exciting. It was beyond a physical attraction, which I always had for him on some level (hard not to, I mentioned the good-looking part, right?). He was everything we are taught to be attracted to — successful, smart, handsome, and available. But it wasn't just that, at least this time. As he walked in, we gave each other a warm hello and the usual hug and kiss on the cheek.

But something was different. It was as if the door pushed wide open in a storm and all the wind, leaves, dirt, and rain rushed through the front door. Something much larger than his 5'10" frame entered. An energetic wave swooped in with him. It was magnetic. It was as if he was transporting a message straight from the heavens. In that moment, the Universe was connecting our energies to show me a new way. It was sending me this person and this exact moment to show me that life could be different. He was a physical representation of what life could be like and what was so clearly missing from my existence today. A smart, successful, seemingly affectionate guy who had his shit together, who dressed to the nines, was free with his compliments, was always kind, and always seemed to light up when he saw me. I don't think my husband had a spark in his eye for me even on our wedding day.

I sat for a while with Dave and my husband as we had dinner and a couple of drinks but I was eager to sneak away and let the two friends have their time together. They stayed up late, talking, laughing, and drinking as they always did. I needed to get into my closet, my sacred space, my sanctuary. I grabbed my journal, which was filling up with writings from my time off, turned on my light and begin processing what was happening. As I wrote, what I was meant to understand about Dave became clearer and clearer.

June 27, 2017

Today I know in the clearest of ways what I am missing. I am missing the true deep in my bones love from a partner. And just as I know I am not the recipient of this type of love, I am also not giving or exuding that type of love toward anyone else, least of all my husband. I have been thinking a lot of love lately. It is a terrible feeling to not be loved. When you are loved unconditionally for all your quirks, all your good habits and even the bad ones, it gives you confidence, it gives you strength and it gives you courage to face all that life brings your way. It also allows you to be really you when you are loved for who you are. So when this type of love is missing, life feels incomplete. On the outside, I have it all. But on the inside, the type of love that I describe is one I do not have. I have no one to blame for this. It is just a fact.

Dave being here during my breakdown was no coincidence. He was meant to show me, teach me, or deliver a message about myself that I was unwilling or unable to realize on my own. What that translated into for me is that I deserved better. I deserved better than this lackluster marriage. I deserved better than being with someone who did not make me feel loved. I deserved better than being with someone who didn't make me feel like my best self. I deserved to be me. I deserved to surround myself with people, situations, places, events, activities that allowed my most authentic self to come to the forefront and remain there happily. I deserved to stop betraying myself, making myself small in order to make someone else big. I deserved to be me. The realest, truest, most authentic version of me. Most importantly, I deserved to feel. I deserved to feel all the physical sensations in my body and all the emotional sensations in my mind. I didn't need to pretend some things didn't matter. I deserved to experience all of life.

I also realized that I was responsible for all this. This was my lesson to learn. I had no one to blame for where I found myself and how I felt. I needed to be true to myself, to my values, to my principles, and to who the Universe put me on this earth to be. I was the one who accepted less. I was the one who made excuses for my husband's behavior or his lack of lovingness towards me. I tolerated situations and behaviors that diminished myself and my worth. That was all on me.

I wrote in an almost frenzied state. The pen flowed on the pages. I couldn't stop it. It was as if I was not the one writing. Something much larger was writing through me. I wrote to the backdrop of my husband and Dave downstairs enjoying their drinks and boisterously reminiscing. I wrote and wrote. As I did, it was becoming clear. I needed to find the path to my truest, most authentic self. I needed to be me again. I needed to pile up the mask, the costume, the playing house, all the fakeness and burn it.

Hello Friend,

It's easy to forget who we are. We don't want to forget. We try to hold onto our own identity but somehow the days, months, years start to pass and as they do for many of us whole parts of our once important selves start to disappear. To get back to who we are takes courage and patience.

To propel me back to who I once was, I started embracing the power of "I am" statements. It is a practice that I learned from watching a sermon delivered by Pastor and Author Joel Osteen. Whatever follows "I am" is what you are giving power too. If I say "I am strong" then I am giving power to my strength by acknowledging and embracing the strength that I have within. The more we focus on what we are or desire to be more of, the more we are inviting that experience into our lives.

Try This   See if you can come up with 10 "I am" statements. Then each morning, review your list. Say each "I am" statement to yourself slowly and clearly. Then each night see if you can add one or two new ones to your list. Here are a couple to get you started: I am loved. I am creative. I am hopeful. I am strong. I am unique. I am blessed. Get the drift? Now it's your turn to give it a try.

Always,
Me

HELLO UNIVERSE, IT'S ME

HELLO UNIVERSE, IT'S ME

SECTION 2: UNDERSTANDING ME
(AND HOW YOU CAN UNDERSTAND YOU TOO)

HELLO UNIVERSE, IT'S ME

CHAPTER 9

Hello Universe,

All that buildup and anticipation and now my breakdown is over. For five months, I thought about what it would be like, how it could play out. But never did I envision it would be even better than I imagined. I mean who wouldn't love to ditch their job and instead spend their days doing yoga, meditating, painting, writing? It was a pretty good gig while it lasted. Oh — and it is totally not lost on me for a second how lucky I am to have the privilege of taking a month off work for this.

Now that it is ending, I realize I gave no consideration to what would happen next. I longed to be in this moment, in my breakdown, experiencing, feeling, breaking down in my own unique way. I wanted to reach deep inside myself, to feel, to understand, to reset, to hear my own truths and to redefine how life needed to look.

I am so grateful for this time to do just that. But now that time is over, how will I wake up from this? How will my life move forward? How will I take the steps necessary to translate all those insights into action? How do I create a life that is authentic and allows me to be the most real version of me?

It is like I have spent these weeks downloading a new software for my life. I have seen the demo of how the new software works, I know it will make my life better, but I don't really know if I have the commitment to fully re-program myself in the ways this software requires. Will I just fall back into old patterns, into old ways of doing things, into what is familiar and known to me?

I know if I work out every day and commit to a new diet, I can change my body (all the diets and workout regimens I have started and stopped over the years prove that). I know that if I pull out all the cleaning supplies and start scrubbing, my house will eventually sparkle. Same must be true for my mind. The way I view the world, the way I live within it, the way I conduct myself, the way I interact with others. It is within my power to change it all, isn't it? I am not just born with a certain disposition and that's it, stuck with that forever. If everything else around us can change — from the weather, the position of the planets, the waves in the ocean, our own physical bodies — then there is absolutely no reason that I can't re-program my mind and change the way I experience my place in this world.

I know with your help, You are going to show me how to do that. You are going to keep hitting the gongs, giving me the signals, the Soul Sparks I need to keep moving in the direction I am meant to go. You helped me hear the message I was meant to hear - to be me. You wanted me to believe in my bones that I cannot, I must not, betray myself anymore. Most importantly, You wanted me to know that You are with me. For that I am so grateful. I am going to show up for myself. I am going to change my life.

Always,
Me

Sitting on the airplane looking out the window at the coastline below, all I could do was smile. It was a quintessential California day and my window seat on the short flight from Los Angeles back to the Bay Area did not disappoint. The sky was a magical shade of majestic blue. There were a few whimsical yet perfectly positioned thin clouds making simple streaks of gentle white in the sky. The plane hugged the coastline as we flew at 30,000 feet. The picturesque waves of the ocean ebbed and flowed in a rhythmic and almost sensual way. There were boats along the coast too. I couldn't quite decipher the type of boats or the size. I could just see their masts glistening against the water's smooth and elegant waves. It was an exquisite, perfectly curated moment by the Universe to soak in all the experiences and insights gained during my time off.

As I admired the scene below, I was overcome with joy. A month ago, when my breakdown began, I would not have noticed the details of what was happening around me. Normally on these flights I would have my laptop open working away on whatever pressing client matter required my attention. I would be consumed with complete tunnel vision on whatever task was in front of me without any regard to where I was or what was happening around me. Not today. Today I just gazed and relished in all the details I could see below me. I was completely present in this moment and an immense amount of gratitude was washing over me as I experienced this.

I felt full. Full of gratitude, full of love, and full of life because in that moment I was completely and totally present in each second of the flight. I was flying back after five days in LA that marked the grand finale of my time off. It was a big, fun, entertaining and all-around wonderful family wedding where I laughed, danced, and enjoyed each moment. Reveling in the fun, I was my most authentic, most wonderful version of me. I dressed up. I wore pretty jewelry. I laughed, I caught up with old friends and with family I hadn't seen in ages. I was in, truly in, those days. I could feel the energy swirling around me. I could feel the love beaming down from the Universe. I could hear so clearly the lessons the Universe was bestowing upon me. I loved it. I loved every minute of it.

This grand finale was perfectly curated by the Universe. It was a big send-off into my new existence. Life would not be the same. I was flying back not just to my house, my job, my regular life — but to a new awareness and a knowingness that I had tapped into the truest version of me. That this version was a gift that these precious weeks of breaking down had allowed to emerge. I needed to bottle up all the magical goodness and keep it close. I needed to hold on to the energy, the love, and the insights that swirled around me over the last month. I needed to hold on to being present, to being grateful, to being clear about what I needed in life. I needed to grasp it as tight as possible so I could return to this magical goodness at any moment when doubt, fear, or sorrow set in. And let's face it, not everything was going to completely transform just because I had a good month. But if I could tap into this feeling, sprinkle that good pixie dust, wave my magic wand, and go back to the wonder that this month provided, I knew that I could handle whatever happened next. At least, that was the hope.

The more I tried to soak in all that this time off afforded me, the more I didn't want to leave this space that I created for myself. I didn't want to leave behind the insights, the clarity, the experiences, the seeing what I was meant to do, how I was meant to experience life. I didn't want all that to just become a distant memory or some story I told people about how I celebrated my 40th birthday.

I wanted all of this to matter. I wanted to change and keep changing. I wanted to move forward and keep moving forward. I wanted to create — passionately, unabashedly, deliberately and with joy — the life I desired.

So it began. I stayed committed to the deliberate creation of my new life. I took all the lessons of my breakdown and, channeling my inner consultant, made a plan to keep the knowingness gained from my time off close to me each and every day of my regular life. I made a plan to pause daily. To take techniques learned on my silent retreat and incorporate them into my daily life — like drowning out the noise by not watching tv, sitting in silence more (even if it was just for a few minutes), meditating at least once a day and even being outside in nature just observing a hummingbird zipping by as I sipped my morning coffee. I made a plan to keep journaling. I made a plan to keep tuning into the Soul Sparks that showed up in my regular everyday life and using them as guideposts to traverse my existence. I made a plan to keep painting and to retain that beautiful feeling of being swept up in my canvases, brushes, and paints. I made a plan to be fiercely committed to every small moment. To knowing that the Universe would present new doors and when it did, I would be perfectly positioned to walk right through them. I made a plan to be focused on seeing the signs but also on letting go and surrendering to what the Universe would bring my way.

I made a plan to let life unfold. To not control it, to not orchestrate it, to not even fully plan for it. I made a new plan to think less and just be more. To release to the Universe my deepest desires and watch the Universe magically return everything I dreamed of to me. What I didn't know is how exactly it would all come to be. But through my breakdown, I realized that I was becoming increasingly comfortable with not knowing. I just had to be fully present in each moment of my day. I had to be willing to see the messages the Universe was sending my way. I had to believe that I could attract into existence all I wanted. If I could embrace the energy of my sabbatical and to my deepest beliefs, then I could just let it all unfold.

I was changing my life's vibration: the rhythm with which I lived and the energy I received, as well as what I transmitted out into the world, was shifting. I learned that when I operated from a place of fear, concern, stress, anxiety and confusion, the energy that reverberated out of me was low, weak, and lethargic. When I operated from a place of hopefulness, joy, empowerment, engagement, and excitement, the energy reverberating out of me was high, positive, strong, and energetic. One of these energy forms is far greater than the other — and I knew clearly that I wanted more of the good kind.

Conceptually, I knew this long ago. Even as kids when we are happy, playing outside, being with our friends, going down that slide, swinging on that swing, enjoying an ice cream. The happiness of those moments radiates like beams of sun touching your skin. Your energy is vibrant, healthy, amazing. But then there is the opposite of those days. The day the cupcake we coveted dropped on the floor and our mother wouldn't get us another one. The day we got punished for scribbling our crayons all over the walls or breaking some other seemingly unnecessary or illogical rule our parents set for us. On those days we were mad, and in our kidlike way we were all-the-way mad. We were emanating madness, throwing fits, crying, stomping around the house. On those days the energy we gave off was low, bad, not the type of energy our parents, our siblings or anyone else wanted to latch on to. We knew even as kids that we felt better when swirling with the positive energy than with the not-so-positive one.

All I wanted to do each day was focus on exuding these high-level vibrations. That way the energy and life that I desired would attract itself to me and me to it. Being in this mindset was a magical uplift to my daily life. I was operating at a joyous and elevated plane. It was unlike anything I had ever experienced.

Hello Friend,

Have you ever returned home from your favorite café and wished you could keep those café vibes going? If you are like me, heading to a local coffee shop is a tiny reprieve from an otherwise hectic day. I want the sensation of sitting at my favorite wooden table, sipping my carefully crafted cappuccino with its foamy heart swirl made by my favorite barista as I lean back, gazing out the window, to carry me through my entire day. Yet within minutes of leaving, that lovely café vibe just fades away as everyday life starts to take over.

Well, perhaps we can consciously attempt to remain connected to whatever feeling, emotion, sensation that you want to cultivate more of by simply giving yourself space and time to nurture it.

Think for a moment about what type of feelings or sensations that you want more of in your life. It can be anything. The joy you feel when sitting in your backyard to marvel at nature. The love you feel when you tuck your kids into bed at night. Really settle into those feelings or sensations that add to your life. The ones that make you feel good. You probably also know what triggers those good feelings for you. Now I want you to sit back and think about how you can actively create more of these good feelings in your life. The more we actively create these feelings, the more we can stay in the vibration that these feelings create. The more we do that deliberately, the more natural it will become.

*Try
This*

Take a piece of paper and write down these positive emotions that you want more of in your life. Next to each positive emotion, write down the activities that trigger them. Carefully examine your list. Are there ways you can incorporate a few of the activities that create that good feeling for you? Is there a way for you to do these activities every day or perhaps every week? Give it a try for five days and reflect on how these changes make you feel. If you are anything like me, finding even a few moments to cultivate more of how you want to feel in your life leads to more of those feelings throughout the day.

*Always,
Me*

CHAPTER 10

Hello Universe,

I now know in the clearest of ways that I cannot be in this marriage. I probably knew this years before the crying sessions in my closet. I knew it long before my breakdown. I probably knew I shouldn't have married my husband before I ever walked down the aisle. I just could never fully admit it to myself. Whenever these thoughts bubbled up before, I would just try to move past the thought as quickly as possible. I glossed over it. I wouldn't give it any attention. It was a far too overwhelming a subject to contemplate, so I never let myself go there. And if I did go there, I wouldn't let myself stay there for too long. It seemed so farfetched, so impractical and just downright hard. I would talk myself out of it and just return to living in a space of dissatisfaction and unhappiness. Maybe it was some form of acceptance that this is the life I had chosen for myself so I had to find a way to live within it.

But I now know for certain that I need to be free of this marriage. Being able to say that is liberating. Up until my scheduled breakdown, I couldn't fully see what was staring me in the face. Even if I did catch glimpses of how unhappy it made me, I couldn't let myself sit with that thought for long.

Not anymore.

But do I have the courage, the guts, to really walk away?

We have been married for over seven years. We have a daughter together. We have a business together. We have a home together. We have a life together. I have no idea how all of this gets dismantled and how something new gets created. All I really know for now is that I am allowing myself to consider this thought in a way that I have never done before.

You have been flashing giant warning signs since before I was ever married. I consciously and continuously made a choice to ignore You. But I see it all now. I am listening now.

Always,
Me

Intention is an aim. It is what you are determined to do, what you are consumed with, what you are putting your attention towards. Creating your best life requires intention. There is no intention too big, too grand, too out of reach. If you can visualize it for yourself, it is absolutely, 100% possible. The tall pile of spiritual books on my bedside table said so and I believed in my bones this was true.

Professional athletes show that you can achieve the seemingly impossible. Whether it is Serena Williams, Michael Jordan, or the U.S. Women's Soccer Team, they knew early on that they wanted to be the very best. They wanted to win. That's it. In other words, they had a clear intention. Long before they were noticed for their athleticism, their skill, their strength, they started leaning all the way into that intention. They began believing in their bones that it is possible for them to be the best. It is in how they walk, how they talk, it occupies their thoughts during the day and fills their dreams at night. They are consumed by this desire.

It is that feeling of which us regular non-athletes catch a glimpse when we watch the sport we love. If you are anything like me, you have imagined yourself as the basketball player dribbling down the court, seconds to go in the game, defenders all over you, yet somehow you find a little space to dribble through, you jump, you shoot, you score! You hear the swoosh of the net, the roar of the crowd, the buzzer indicating the game is over and that you won. You are that player celebrating unabashedly, the one whose teammates hoist up into the air for getting them the victory.

Athletes tell everyone who will listen — their coaches, their teammates, their friends, their family, their fans — that they will be the best at their sport.

They grow singularly focused on doing only those things that help them win. That means finding the best coach, making time to hit the gym to get stronger, eating the right foods, training and everything else they need to do to have more endurance, to run faster, to jump higher, to hit the ball harder, to kick farther. To be the best.

When these athletes play, they solely focus on getting that ball where it needs to go. They aren't thinking about where they are going to dinner afterwards, what they are wearing or how they look on TV. They are focused on being in that game and winning it. If they aren't focused on the game at hand, what happens? They don't win. They don't play their best.

If it works for athletes to reach the pinnacles of their sports, it undoubtedly was gonna work for me, too. I knew that when I did focus, I saw results, whether studying for a test I wanted to ace or interviewing for my dream job. If I focused on it, prepared for it wholeheartedly, performed my best and really in my heart believed that it would be mine, I achieved it.

The shifts I wanted to make now were far greater. I needed to figure out how to totally and completely transform the life I was living. I needed to create the space I needed to live my best life. This required an unwavering commitment and I finally felt prepared to do it. I should say it was a *mostly* unwavering commitment because in the months that followed there was some wavering and confusion that took hold, which, by the way, is totally normal and should be anticipated.

So I decided to pray. My bedroom was already my sanctuary, but now that my husband had started sleeping in a different room, I could come out of the closet and make the whole space my sanctuary. I could play soothing music. I could light my candles. I could meditate. I could read religious and spiritual texts. I could even proudly display crystals without fear that I would be discovered or questioned. I created my own little oasis. Each night in that oasis, after I put my daughter to sleep, I would sit up in bed, clasp my hands together and pray. I would pray for the Universe to show me the way.

I started by making my intentions clear. What was the aim? What was I determined to do? What would I courageously, consciously, and deliberately put my attention towards? The answer: giving myself full permission to be my most authentic self. It was creating a life that was completely and totally authentic and let myself be the truest version of me. It was a life where I was not pretending, where I was not playing house. Where I was not small. Where I was not undervalued. Where I was not expecting so little from others. Rather, it was a life where I honored my inner home, my inner heart, my inner essence that for all the years of my marriage was locked away in a cabinet and the key was nowhere to be found. It was also time to fully acknowledge that this crappy marriage didn't happen to me. I contributed to creating a life, a marriage and a home that was the antithesis of anything I ever knew or wanted. I contributed to living a life that masked my own true feelings. I behaved in ways that allowed myself to be small. I accepted that role in my marriage. This is not a he-was-all-wrong and I-was-all-right situation. To be my fully authentic self, I needed to recognize this and accept it. While I hadn't formed in my mind what that authenticity would look like exactly, I knew that authenticity is what I needed to bring to the forefront of my life. That was the aim. That was my bulls-eye.

At first the intention felt too big, too grand, too abstract. It just seemed so unattainable. Not at all practical. Wouldn't it be easier to intend to be thin or intend to go on a vacation to the Bahamas? Having an intention towards something tangible or that I could get with a credit card seemed so much more practical then something as abstract as being authentic and living a life of love.

As these questions were swirling in my head, I was mindlessly surfing the channels on the TV and came across Iyanla Vanzant. She is an inspirational speaker, spiritual teacher and life coach who is frequently featured on Oprah's OWN network, which was the channel I landed on in that moment. Oprah was interviewing Iyanla. I heard Iyanla's powerful voice bravely say with the flair of a Southerner in church, *"If God gave you the vision, he will give you the provision.*" In that moment my mindless channel surfing transformed into a Soul Spark. I sat up on the couch, turned up the volume and listened to Oprah and Iyanla talk about their spiritual beliefs. It was two gal pals speaking directly to me and all the spiritual concepts that I was grappling with. It was a conversation tailor-made for me.

That Soul Spark, courtesy of Oprah and Iyanla, bubbled up the greatest sensation within me. If I could see it, I could achieve it. There is no intention too big or too out of reach. You can set an intention for absolutely anything. The possibilities are limitless. I sat on my couch feeling giddy. Like I had uncovered some magical secret. You want a house in the mountains? It's possible. You want a tall, dark and handsome man to sweep you off your feet? It's possible. You want to have your financial stressors go away? It's possible. Oprah and Iyanla confirmed that the desires women like me were sometimes to afraid to even whisper out loud should really be screamed from the rooftops. They should be embraced. And if we can catch a glimpse of them, no matter how tiny, they can in fact be our reality. No matter how farfetched it may seem.

The only way that I was going to make my intention a reality was to unleash myself from the confines of my marriage. Terrifying. When I say that, I mean a big-burly-dude-with-a-mask-entering-your-home-in-the-middleof-the-night-waving-a-machete type of terrifying.

While I occasionally thought about what it would be like to not be in this marriage, I never fully let myself consider it. I would think about it after a fight with my husband. I would think about it when I couldn't sleep. I would think about it when I saw other couples in a loving embrace. I would think about it at dinner parties where my husband would be the life of a party, while I sat alone in a corner. I would think about it even sitting with my husband on the couch not saying much to each other. Nothing about our relationship ever felt right to me. Ever. Not while we were married. Not when we were dating. Not even the day I walked down the aisle. Yet here I was married for seven plus years with a beautiful little daughter. I was totally and completely lost in my world, pretending to be someone else around my husband to not rock the boat on the world we had created.

To not be married, or worse, to be divorced, was a frightening space for me. I was a product of an intact nuclear family. My mom and dad were married for more than 30 years before my dad passed away. My parents, my brother, sister, and I lived together in the same house until each of us left for college. That's all I knew about family: Dad picked you up from school every day, watched MTV after school with you (he knew all the hip-hop songs and he would even sing along), Mom came home and made dinner, and then we watched Peter Jennings and discussed the day's news together. Every single evening. It was the same routine with different MTV songs, different dinners, different news, and different anchors. It was not just quality time we spent together — laughing, eating, talking — but also quantity time. We were always together as a family and that was wondrous.

I couldn't visualize my daughter not having the type of upbringing that I did. Yet, I also recognized clearly that she wasn't experiencing anything like it no matter how hard I tried. She came home to an exhausted mother who was overwhelmed but always trying her best. She came home to a mother who was still taking conference calls and pounding away on her laptop. She came home to three different dinners — one for her, one for Mom and one for Dad — since we could never agree on what to eat and what time to eat it. She came home to parents who were so disenchanted with one another that they hardly spoke and mostly communicated through her. Like *"Pumpkin, tell Papi that we are going for a play date tomorrow"* Or me saying *"Momma will be late coming home tonight"* in clear earshot of my husband.

I, on the other hand, grew up with parents who loved each other. Dad's eyes would sparkle every time Mom walked in a room. My Mom and Dad were the epitome of a team, working together in almost perfect unison. Through good times and downright terrible times, it was the same. They were verbal and forceful in their love for each other and for their children. We felt their love for each other and for us in our bones. Even when there was an argument, they moved past it swiftly. There was no blame, no grudges. Just a quick return to leading their days with love. That love fueled an atmosphere in our home of confidence, security, and freedom to be who we were and live our best lives. It emanated from the walls, from the furniture, from the ceilings. Everyone could feel it when they entered our home. There was something magical going on between the walls.

Fast forward to my marriage, where none of that felt present. Instead it left me insecure, uncomfortable, unloved, and a shadow of the person I had once been. I was constantly pretending, faking it, acting. When the three of us were together, our house had an atmosphere that was just blah. There was no magic-making happening here. It was a place of heaviness, a lack of authenticity, and just downright stasis.

I didn't share my dreams and aspirations the way my dad so freely and eagerly did with my mom. I didn't share the happenings of my day the way my mom did with my dad from the minute she plopped her purse down after a long day at work. There was no point. My husband's reaction was never what I expected nor what I hoped for.

Take the time I came home after having the most wonderful day at work. The kind of day that that you see in your favorite movie or TV show. The one where I saved the day by making the absolute perfect pitch to an important client. The kind of day where everyone was giving me high-fives after the meeting and realizing how valuable I was to the team. I came home on a high. I was feeling vibrant, excited, proud, and just all- around wonderful. I saw my husband and, with so much enthusiasm, I said, *"You know, I think I can be a CEO someday."*

He just laughed and retorted, *"Who on earth would hire you as a CEO?"* I felt my stomach clench and tears form behind my eyes. He added, *"You don't have any of the qualities it would take."* He then proceeded to give me a litany of traits that I lacked. He went through each one as if he were mocking me. That hurt.

Instead of having incidents like this occur over and over, the dynamic with my husband shifted to that of meaningless chit-chat about the weather, the accident on the freeway, or whatever current event was on the news. The most meaningful topic in our house was logistics related to our daughter (what time she ate, when she slept, how good or bad her poop was). The lack of confidence and intimacy that was the norm of our marriage created an environment devoid of sharing freely. How it started and why it never changed, I do not fully understand.

If I could not create the feeling of my childhood when my husband was around, I certainly tried my best to do it whenever my daughter and I were alone, just the two of us. We would turn on the music and bust into a crazy dance party or set up our easels outside to paint, create, share, and talk for hours painting in the sun. Or we would just whisper secrets to each other which mostly involved one of us saying *I love you more, more, more* until we couldn't say it without laughing.

I knew that my daughter's upbringing was nothing like my own. Her parents didn't interact in healthy ways. My relationship with my husband and even the structure of our family life was nothing like what I'd known. It was not a structure that brought out the best in each of us. It was not deeply loving, confidence-creating, there was no sense of team, no sense that we were in this together, no sense that we were making something amazing as a unit. Instead, we were three people operating completely and totally separately under one roof.

I knew this relationship needed to change. I was fairly certain that it wasn't going to correct course or magically get better. I left the idea of it getting better behind years ago when I would plead with my husband to go to couples counseling, which he always refused. What I longed for was the idea of being extracted from the confines of this marriage to live a life of love. If I was really going to return to my best, most authentic, and real self, then I needed to be free of a relationship and a life that had weighed me down so heavily.

Hello Friend,

I offer you this space as a place for you to set your intention. Even if you have never set an intention before, even if you have no idea what intention to set, I offer you this moment to think about it freely and openly.

Try This *Sit out in nature or in your favorite cozy chair in your house. Get quiet. Turn off the TV, the iPads, the phone and whatever other devices zips, zaps, or buzzes in your world. Sit with yourself in this quiet space for a few moments. Feel free to close your eyes and take a few deep breaths if that feels comfortable to you.*

Once you feel like you have slowed down and have gotten to a place of calm and quiet, pose this question to yourself: If you had no restrictions, no limitation and you knew you would succeed, what step would you take right now in your life? It can be anything at all. If you knew you would be able to achieve it, what would you do?

Whatever thought elevates to the top of the heap in that moment of quiet, sit with it and be curious about it. Don't judge, assess, or evaluate. Instead, try being inquisitive. Try poking around this thought and contemplating it further. Be open to diving into it and why it emerged for you.

This may or may not be the intention for you, but if you ask your deepest self about what intentions you should hold and what you should be leaning into, an answer is bound to emerge.

Be curious about that.

Always.
Me

CHAPTER 11

Hello Universe,

You better have some answers for me now because I am starting to panic. The scheduled breakdown was amazing. The insights were abundant and all-around fantastic but, wow, this intention feels really big. Who am I to have an intention this big? Who am I to believe that this can be real? What on earth am I thinking? Why am I even thinking it? And even if it can be real, am I sure I really want this?

In this moment, I am crazed with fear. Overwhelmed by it. I simply don't know what to do. I cry. I feel deep sadness. I feel so unprepared to steer this ship in the right direction. When my fear gets the better of me, I try to recall all the teachings and insights I gained during my breakdown. I know that meditation, journaling, painting, and yoga came into my awareness to help me deal with these times when I feel like I can't or shouldn't believe in myself.

When the fear subsides enough for me to have a clear thought, I understand that changing my life is big. Upending what I know about myself and my world is big. Something this big should feel unsettling at some level. Still, if this desire to change my life keeps trying to get my attention I guess somehow, someway, You will show me what to do with this. You will guide me, direct me, point me in the direction on how this all becomes a reality, right? I am trying not to intellectualize. I am trying not to let my practical side get in the way of this creation. I am trying to subdue the self-doubt making its way in. My scheduled breakdown showed me in the clearest of ways that there is a better way and I need to use my treasured tools — the journaling, the yoga, the meditation, the silence — to get me past these fears so I can keep operating from a more elevated spiritual plane and leave my logical mind on the sidelines.

But geez, Universe, that day is not today. I am trying but I am so, so, so scared.

Always,
Me

It is scary to lean into your intention. If anyone says *"it's so natural"* or *"it was effortless,"* check their nose because it will be growing long as Pinocchio. Letting yourself dream and believe in a drastically different life is not easy. It is terrifying with a capital T, underlined, bold, exclamation point times 10! For some of us, just the act of formulating a vision or intention in our minds of what we want for ourselves can feel scary. When you layer in that this vision and intention can actually become your life — that, my friend, is downright frightening.

It is frightening because you are going to wonder loudly and often if you are even worthy of what you are striving towards. Do you deserve what it is you are wishing for? Spoiler alert! You are wholeheartedly, completely, and totally deserving of anything you can imagine in your life. If you can see it, even if it is just a tiny glimpse, you are being given that vision because you do deserve it. You are absolutely, 100% deserving of all you see for yourself.

Even bigger than wondering if you deserve it, is the frightening thought that not only *could* it happen, but what if all of this *does* happen? It means life as you know it today will be dramatically different. It will change. It will transform. Life will deliver to you the better circumstances, situations, or people that you desire and that you deserve. All of this because you saw a new way of being, you set your intention, and you spent your time believing it could be so. What you are wishing for will prevail. Imagine that. Imagine that the intention or vision you have for yourself is your reality.

It's scary because you already know how to be unhappy. You have lived in this place of unhappiness for so long. You understand it. You know how to be in that unhappy rhythm. It is familiar to you. You are strangely more comfortable staying in this unhappy place because you know everything about this unhappiness and how to survive within it. You know how this unhappiness feels when you wake up, how it feels as you move through your day. You know how it feels at night as you go to bed. Being unhappy and living in that space is part of you. As much as on some level you dislike it, hate it, despise it, feel crushed by the weight of it, it is what you know and what you know is familiar. It's hard to break from what feels comfortable and familiar, no matter how terrible or toxic that familiar place may be.

This was the certainly the case for me. On the one hand it was exciting to think about living an authentic life full of love. Sign me up. Sounds fantastic. Beam me up into that, Scotty. On the other hand, it was scary to conceive of how I would untangle from the life I was living to experience that future life. It was scary to contemplate how topsy-turvy life would undoubtedly have to become to make that new life a reality.

I caught glimpses of this new life. In the evenings, as my husband would pour himself a scotch and offer me a glass of wine, the conversation would slip into life logistics, my least favorite topic. *"Hey, this bill is due. Can you transfer money into the joint account?"* Or *"Did you notice the electric bill is too high? We need to use less AC."* I despised these conversations. We seemed to never get past logistics. I know they are needed, but there had to be more for us to talk about than bills. We never discussed our dreams or aspirations. Heck, we didn't even discuss politics or the events of the day. We certainly never talked about living our most authentic and truthful lives.

It was in these no-nothing conversations when I would close my eyes and transport myself into a more dynamic, fun, engaging and all-around interesting conversation with an imaginary boyfriend in my head. I would let myself daydream about what I wished was transpiring in my life. I would imagine myself in a place where I didn't feel bogged down by life logistics but rather inspired by fun-loving, interactive, and uplifting talk. The type of talk that I so desired to have with my husband but just never seemed to happen.

DEEPIKA SANDHU

I was no longer interested in what lit him up. I was no longer interested in what was fun for him. I was not interested in how he could live his best life. I was run down by a relationship that didn't deliver this for me. As I lost myself, I lost interest in him. So I dreamed up a new relationship. The new imaginary relationship made me smile. It made me giddy. It made me happy. It made me full. It was becoming my intention to realize this new reality. But just as soon as my daydream would fill me with joy, I would quickly be brought down to earth as I thought through all that needed to be dismantled, broken, torn apart for my imaginary life to be my reality.

If my intention was to win the lottery and then I did, that would just be excitement. Winning the lottery does not seem to encompass any negatives. Seems like an all-around positive occurrence. Have more money. Eliminate all financial fears. Quit job. Go on oodles of fancy vacations to exotic locations.

But my intention was to transform my life to a place where I operated from love and lived as my most authentic self. What did that mean? To be honest, in that moment that this realization landed in my awareness, I had no idea what it meant. All I knew is that these words were surfacing. They were Soul Sparks. Heck, it was more like a Soul Forest Fire because I couldn't shake the thought. These words were not hollow. They were full of meaning that I was yet to uncover. They were words that had to be unwrapped and understood to become my new reality.

To make that a reality would be a big shift. Whenever, I let my brain start thinking about how that would happen or when that would happen, the fear would kick into overdrive. I had so much fear of flipping all that was normal to me on its head to make some new, possibly far-flung, possibly foolish, possible really-bad-for-me-idea into a reality.

Along with the fear came a double dose of self-doubt that I begin to refer to as my saboteur. There were countless moments when I let my saboteur right in the front door with a red-carpet welcome when I really should have kicked the door shut and not let that the little devil anywhere near me.

My saboteur was an intimidating bouncer standing with hands folded in front of the hottest new nightclub, giving me that *look* that said I was not good enough to get in. The bouncer that stares you up and down and makes you question if you picked the right dress, wore the right makeup, or curled your hair enough. My saboteur stood in my way. He was a nagging voice whispering negativity in my ear. My saboteur always worked overtime twisting and turning scenarios around in my mind, making me doubt myself, my desires, my life. Not only did they enter through my ears and move into my brain, but they settled in.

My saboteur was insistent about how terrible I was for even desiring a change. *Why was I not happy? I had it all — The nice house, the nice cars, nice clothes, nice vacations, the picturesque family. What about this was not making me happy? What would this do to my daughter? Did I want to be responsible for messing up her life? My husband could get better. He could change. Seven years wasn't long enough for people to change. Give him seven more years and something was bound to get better. Plus, you could change too. You could be more accepting of him. You could change your expectations. You could be nicer to his friends. You could work less and be home more to keep working on the marriage. Or you could work even more and be home even less to avoid dealing with him. You could lose weight. You could cut your hair. You can find ways to be more attractive to him. That could change things.* Why would I need to leave this marriage when there clearly were fixes I could make?

The self-doubt had to stop. I spent my whole life listening to the saboteur and feeding my own insecurities and I did not want to do that anymore. I decided that while I couldn't stop the saboteur from muttering a word (he had been around so long, he wasn't going to go away that easily), I could recognize when he started talking and before he started stirring the cauldron of fear and self-doubt too much, I could kindly tell my saboteur that I appreciated his input, but I was no longer interested in listening. I focused on becoming aware of when the saboteur was present. I consciously recognized that he was popping in to sow his seeds of self-doubt. I would let him talk for a bit. I didn't avoid him. I knew from his long tenure in my life that he wasn't going away with a snap of a finger. I just started to not let him go on very long.

I treated my saboteur as a friend. The kind of friend who is texting incessantly about their issues and problems. The kind of friend you sometimes need to tell *"Busy right now but you got this, girl ...talk in a few!"* We ALL have that friend. In the kindest of ways, I started acknowledging the presence of my saboteur and what he was saying, but actively chose not to feed his thoughts in any way. I even gave it a nickname. I named my saboteur Minmi (the name of the type of dinosaur my daughter and I liked the most and always giggled about as we read our Dinosaur Encyclopedia). Whenever Minmi would get going, I would say: *"There, there, Minmi. I know you have so much to say, but for now, I am just going to ask you to be a good pet and sit in this little corner. I have bigger things to do today and we will get to you and your concerns another time."* No joke. This is what I did. Time and again. Minmi would start spewing the crazy. I would realize it was happening. I would shut it down kindly by acknowledging it had something to say and that we could discuss it all later.

Minmi needed to be acknowledged. He needed to know that I wasn't trying to avoid it or ignore it. He needed to know that he was in fact part of me and who I was. He was the part of me that was concerned, that responded to fear. We need this part in our life. We need it when there are situations that should cause concern or fear such as when you're walking alone at night and two men start running toward you. Be concerned. Be very concerned! We need it in that moment so our brain can figure out how to walk the other direction or take some sort of action to be safe in that moment.

Fears are okay, too. It is okay to be afraid when you are about to touch a hot pot. You should be afraid of that hot pot as it could burn your hand if you touch it. These feelings of fear, concern and worry have a place in our life, but that place isn't when you are trying to create what is best for you. It is not when a fear has become so ingrained in you that it is derailing your ability to work in your best interest. I decided to deliberately and consciously pay far less attention to these feelings. When the self-doubt, the worry, the fear would creep in and that saboteur would start talking in my ear, my first strategy was to recognize that he was indeed talking. Then, I consciously opt to reserve the feelings bubbling up for a different time. I actively moved away from the feelings I didn't want to have and moved towards more of the feelings that I did want to have.

This is how I learned to control my thoughts. I began to embrace the Law of Attraction. It contends that we get more of what we think about. If I could spend my time thinking of whatever I wanted in my life, according to the Law of Attraction, I would actively attract those thoughts into becoming reality. If I wrapped myself up in thoughts of negativity, of self-doubt, of not being deserving — guess what would happen? My world would create more situations that are negative, that promote the self-doubt and more belief that I do not deserve any better. If I could instead start to think more about what could be, then all that could be — the possibilities, the dreams, the intentions, the manifestations — would come about.

This is not simple, and it certainly isn't going to happen overnight. That said, if you want to achieve that beautiful vision you have for yourself, then you have to actively, deliberately, and conscientiously move away from the stories we all repeat, creating more negativity and less of the places we wish to find ourselves.

Hello Friend,

If you are like me, no matter how much outward confidence you exude and no matter how good your life may look to others, feelings such as doubt, anxiety, worry, and fear are present. For some, those feelings take hold, and they can be paralyzing.

There is no simple way to remove these feelings, but we do not have to indulge them. Pay them less mind. They may not leave you completely, but if we deliberately and consciously feed those negative thoughts less and feed the positive thoughts more, tangible shifts in our life can occur.

Try This

When the feelings of anxiety, self-doubt, fear take hold, try asking the Universe for an intuitive hit. Create a sacred space and find as much quiet as you can. You may want to light a candle, play some soft or soothing music. Get completely comfortable in that quiet. Sit on a chair, sit cross-legged on the floor, maybe lay flat on your bed. Get in the most comfortable position you can find. Take a few deep breaths. Put your hands on your belly and literally feel your belly rise and fall with each inhale and exhale. Do this for a few minutes and really be present and aware with these breaths. Then when you feel deep within this space, I invite you to talk to the Universe. Your request may go something like this:

"Universe, I am open to your guidance and excited to receive what you are giving me. Universe, join with me to co-create the clearest intuitive understanding of my next step."

As you make this request, imagine that you are releasing it. Picture it as a helium balloon. Watch it release into the sky. Try not to actively wait for a response or worry about when a response is coming. The work you just did in asking for guidance and releasing it is powerful. The Universe will respond.

Always,
Me

CHAPTER 12

Hello Universe,

I'm scared. I think the high from my time off has officially come to an end. The realities of life are popping up again. It's confusing, overwhelming, and far less enjoyable than that glorious month off. I just don't know how to take all those amazing insights and make them part of my reality. I mean it's one thing to say I will meditate daily, write in my journal, take time to be quiet, and watch the hummingbirds with my coffee — but it is quite another to do them in regular everyday life.

While it feels AH-MAY-ZING to have received all these downloads from You, I am terrified that I won't have the courage and commitment to make them happen. I am scared that the way I want to live just won't work or that I will give up or that I'll do something wrong while trying to make things right.

Yet the other part of me knows that I got this far because I was meant to get this far. I was meant to see that life could be different. I know you will keep offering Soul Sparks to guide me in the right direction. I know I just need to take a deep breath, sit back, and let the insights flow.

Always,
Me

It is one thing to realize that you need to return to your truest, most authentic self and it is quite another to *become* that person. Coming out of my scheduled breakdown, once the euphoria of changing my life started to wane, a wave of confusion and a tinge of sadness came over me as I realized I would need to exchange my paintbrushes, journaling, and meditating for my laptop, client meetings and PowerPoint presentations. Magical as my breakdown was and as perfect as its finale proved, now began my real life. I was no longer free to do as I saw fit all day. Now I had to layer in the confines of my job. I had to layer in the commuting, the meetings, the reviewing of documents, and all that *talking* — talking to clients, talking to my team, talking to folks around the office. Over the last month, I had gotten used to only really talking to my daughter, my husband, the guy at the coffee shop who took my order, and occasionally my mom. The regular routine of my days was returning.

I tried to console myself with the knowledge that even if my breakdown was the *eat-a-tub-of-ice-cream-on-the-couch* variety or the *stay-in-bed-all-weekend-crying-my-eyes-out* type or even the *watch-When-Harry-Met-Sally-on-repeat* breakdown, there would be some relief but also some confusion about how to proceed. While I felt immense gratitude for having experienced this month of inner quiet, self-reflection, and heightened mindfulness, I really didn't know how all of this would translate to my normal, everyday life. I knew I would pause more. I knew I would journal more. I knew I would take more time for me. But how would I truly return to my most authentic self? And even if I could return to it, how would my life change?

One day, a week or so after I returned to work, as I drove home in bumper-to-bumper traffic, I noticed the other drivers in the cars next to me. The man to my right in a white sedan looked haggard, as if something heavy, a financial burden perhaps, was wearing on his mind. The woman to my left in a beige minivan looked worn out too. She was tired from a long day at work and worried that with all this traffic she would be late picking up her kids at daycare. She also didn't know what was for dinner. At least, that is what I imagined was happening with her. Then there was the guy behind me who had his windows rolled down of an old silver Honda Civic. He seemed to be yelling on the phone. Not sure what was going on with him. I would see people like this every day. Tired, unhappy, seemingly unsatisfied. All sitting in traffic just like me. But I didn't want to be just one of these people going through the motions of life. I didn't want to be tired, unhappy, or unsatisfied anymore. I could and would change my life.

I needed to get to work.

It was time to be a super-manifester. All the people, the situations and the circumstances that emerged in my life confirmed that I needed to create the life that I desired. A life that was true to me. I just needed to harness all that I was learning to make this creation a reality. Just like a superhero who becomes aware of their secret superpowers, I was about to use everything in my newly-created tool chest to manifest my very best life.

I moved through my day like I had a secret. Like I knew something no one around me knew. That I could change everything. That night when I opened my journal, the first words on the page were:

July 2017

If I doubted myself before, I do not doubt myself now. Not only can I do it. Universe, I will do it. I know life is never going to be the same.

Life showed me how. It required setting intentions, believing that those intentions could be true, enjoying long periods of silence to hear what my soul wanted me to hear, seeing the signs the Universe presented to me in plain sight, and following my deepest heart's desires to make the life I wanted a reality. Along the way, I needed to be present and grateful in each moment. Immense, inane, overflowing gratitude for absolutely everything: the tree and its branches, the smile on a stranger's face, the dog that stopped me in my tracks for a loving pet, even the bad days, the sad moments, the times I would find myself wallowing in self-pity, because that didn't go away just because I was trying not to feel that way.

Most importantly, I needed to do all of this deliberately. I knew that at some level saying out loud, admitting to myself what I wanted and needed would feel unnatural. Leaning into those newfound truths and believing in them enough so they could become reality was going to feel unnatural too. It would feel contrived. Maybe even forced. But if I wanted to get to a point where all these practices felt natural, organic, and inane, then I had to start by doing them.

That required little Post-It note reminders on my laptop and on my bathroom mirror. It required apps on my phone that reminded me to pause daily, take some deep breaths, get up and walk around, laugh, jump, feel grateful. I literally was setting reminders to prompt me to do all these new activities that I knew would change my life. And I kept doing it until it became second nature.

I also realized that to be a super-manifester, I needed to let go of time and self-doubt. The Universe had to do its work, to rearrange the order of things to create what was meant to be. It required unwavering faith that what was meant to emerge in my life would appear at just the right time. I could not force the timing. I just needed to let it come about. This is a terribly difficult concept, especially for someone like me. My life is on a schedule. I organize my days to a tee. Heck, I am the one who even scheduled time to breakdown! How was I ever going to embrace not knowing when the Universe would deliver all that I asked for?

Well before I was fully cognizant of any spiritual principle and years before my scheduled breakdown, I wanted to get pregnant. I wanted to have a baby so deeply, so intensely, that I was prepared to rock the foundation of my life to make it happen. First, we tried the old-fashioned way — just normal sexy time. When that didn't work, we considered other options — medication, alternative therapies, insemination. Each month, I checked for my period, hoping it didn't come, hoping that this time, this month, it finally worked. And each month that it didn't happen, after trying and trying, I was devastated, heartbroken, exhausted, frustrated, hopeless. I did all the supposedly right things by going to the doctor, getting checkups, taking the medications. But in the end, I didn't control the timing. I couldn't make it happen. I just could not. What is meant for us only transpires when the timing is exactly right. There is a larger life force at work — it is on its own schedule. But when you desire something so completely and totally, it will happen.

Through this tireless practice, I learned that the absolute best happenings only ever came about when it was absolutely and totally meant to. I had no choice but to let everything unfold as it was destined to. If I didn't, I would sabotage all that I was trying to create. I had to accept that the Universe has its own timing. It doesn't follow our schedule on what should happen and when it should happen. You can't speed it up. You can't slow it down. You just keep believing.

Not only is it not going to happen on your timeline, it also may not be in the packaging that you expect. What I want, what is best for me in this life, may not look exactly like the picture in my head. It may not be wrapped exactly the way I envisioned it. But if I focus my energy and emit the frequencies of all that I desire, what I wish for will emerge in a way that is better than I could dream up. My own desires for myself are limited by what I can see, know, or have experienced. The Universes' are not.

I also learned that I could not question what was happening. Would things change? When? How? I just learned to accept that it would. Think of it like those home makeover shows where the couple leaves the house for a week and the designers reimagine the couple's space without consulting them on any detail. The couple almost always loves the house in the end because it is better than they imagined. The how of it all was meant to remain a wondrous mystery until the magical moment of reveal. And as hard as it is to have unwavering faith and be detached from how changes would come, I knew that I needed to believe that the way it was coming about is completely and totally as designed.

Hello Friend,

Have you ever had a moment where you wanted something so deeply, so intensely that you were prepared to rock the foundation of your life to make it happen? It could be the person you wanted to become your significant other, the job you felt would spark an amazing career or even the perfect dream house in the right neighborhood, in the right school district that would strengthen your family. Whatever it is, most of us have experienced some sort of desire that we felt we could not live without.

But what if I told you that you didn't need to be focused on the object — the boyfriend, the job, the house — but rather the feeling that the object represented for you? What are the feelings or sensations that you experience when you feel the presence of these objects — boyfriend, dream job, perfect house — in your life? Is it a feeling of support and security? A feeling of stability? Of love? Does it represent a feeling of freedom?

Rather than fixating in on the vision of what you want, consider focusing in on the feeling that vision creates. It's like listening to music. Music evokes a feeling. Whatever genre you enjoy, music has a magical way of relaxing, inspiring, transporting, or just making us feel our emotions deeply. It is these feelings that we want to cultivate more of in our life.

Try This

Pick a favorite song. One that pleases you, excites you. Perhaps one that makes you dance. Pump up the music. Let the music move you. Dance, sway, shimmy, jump. Really dance. Really feel that song in every inch of your body. Enjoy the music fully. Allow it to take over.

Dancing in that energy is what you want your life to mirror. You want your life to bring to you the same kind of energy, sensation, pleasure, and fun, that you experience when you let yourself just dance it out to your favorite tune.

Knowing what your intention feels like means that when it appears you will know it is here! It may not be packaged in the way you envision it, but the way it makes you feel will be confirmation that all you desired has in fact shown up in this life for you. So pump up the music, lean into that feeling and know that when you dance in that energy that energy will reverberate back to you.

Always,
Me

CHAPTER 13

Hello Universe,

There are so many examples of times when I have thought so much about something that it just became my reality. Like going to my first-choice college. From the day I stepped on the pristine campus of Scripps College with its rolling lawns and picturesque buildings, I knew this is where I wanted to be. From that first visit to campus, I believed that this small liberal-arts school would be the place where the magic of college would unfold for me. Every time I opened my eyes in the morning and right before I went to bed every night, I imagined being there. I imagined myself walking amidst the trees, sitting in the intimate classrooms, going to the parties on campus. I just believed so deeply that I would go to this school. I leaned into this belief every day until I was accepted.

But getting into my first-choice college was different than the changes I am trying to make now, right? Back then, if I was a qualified candidate — the right grades, the right SAT's, the right extracurriculars — I would likely get in. Now even if I do everything right, I could still fail. But I don't want to fail. I want to believe in myself the way I did back then. I need to believe in my bones that the changes I want to make now, the life I want to live and the way I want to live it can indeed be mine.

I know I need to lessen the voices of self-doubt. Just please keep giving me the courage to believe wholeheartedly. I know believing, like really believing, is the path to manifesting a new life where I could be my truest self.

Keep pushing me along.

Always,
Me

What beliefs have you held? Like wholeheartedly, unwaveringly, in your gut, no one could tell you otherwise, believed. For me, the last time that happened was with Santa Claus. The jig with Santa is intense. From as early as I can remember, until about the age of seven, I believed in him. I was all in on this and so were my parents. Even though my Mom and Dad were immigrants and come from a culture where Santa Claus did not enjoy the VIP status he does in Western society, they were both committed to making sure our upbringing was like all the other families in our area. We had a Christmas tree filled with beautiful ornaments, which had presents underneath, perfectly wrapped and waiting for us to tear through on Christmas morning. We watched all the Christmas specials on TV together. We stood in line at the mall to sit on Santa's lap and take a picture like all the other kids in our neighborhood. And we always drove around town after dark to see the exquisite light displays on the houses and tall buildings. Oh — and don't even get me started on how much our family loved eggnog.

Then one day, seemingly out of the blue, when I least expected it, my mean older cousin let it slip that Santa wasn't real. She was the one who always forced me into playing WWF-style wrestling. She was 9 and I was 7. She headbutted me (typical sneaky WWF move) and body-slammed me onto the bed, which was our makeshift wrestling ring. That's when she blurted out that Santa wasn't real. I remember the shock and sadness amidst the daze and confusion. I went straight to my parents who were casually sipping tea with my Auntie and Uncle in the living room. I will never forget the expressions on their faces in that moment. They all smiled. Adults do that when you discover what they already knew.

How could something that I believed in so passionately, so fully, so completely, be fake? No Santa, no elves, no toy shop in the North Pole, no Dasher, no Rudolph, no coming down the chimney. All of it was a lie. The toys were from China and the person eating the cookies and milk on Christmas Eve after I went to sleep was my Dad.

Yet when my 40-year-old self struggled to really believe in my intentions, the feeling that I kept going back to was how my younger self felt about Santa. I needed to believe in my intentions now the way I believed back then that Santa was going to deliver that sparkly new My Little Pony on Christmas morning. Back then, I had no fear. No doubts. I knew I had been nice, not naughty, and that if I held onto the Christmas spirit, the feeling of the season and believed that I would get the toy that I desired.

I needed to tap into that feeling now. There was no room for fear that my intentions would not materialize. There was no room to be scared about how different life might be if it happened. No time for sadness that my beliefs would not become my reality.

The problem was that it had been 33 years since I believed in Santa. The day-to-day commotion of life buried my ability to believe and it buried it deep. The reality is that after Santa there were countless events in my life that I hoped for, prayed for, literally sat in temple and begged God for, that just didn't happen. The boyfriend that never proposed. The job that I thought would change everything — and that I didn't get. The ailing friend that I hoped would walk out of the hospital one day but never did. Life can crush us. We begin to accept disappointments. Struggle becomes what life is all about.

Yet, I knew that that there were countless times in my life where I really did believe — and what I believed in *happened*. Most of those times were in my youth, but I know that it existed and if it existed once, it could exist again. I needed to foster that feeling within myself now. I needed to tap into that magic, that hope, that belief. I needed to tap into the unwavering faith the little girl in me had for Santa Claus, the Tooth Fairy, and whatever else I believed in as a kid. I didn't need to be skeptical. I didn't need to ask and answer 1000 *what-could-go-wrong-type* questions. I didn't need to fill myself with paralyzing levels of self-doubt. I just needed to *believe*. No matter how difficult that felt, no matter how farfetched, I just needed to believe.

Then came a regular, ordinary day. My daughter and I were on our usual 8:30 AM drive to her school. We were talking our silly talk as we admired the birds, the trees, the random bright yellow car that zipped by. We were singing too, as we did most days. I would encourage her to sing softly in a whisper and other times we would be extra silly, roll the windows down and sing as loud as we could. Both versions of our singing made us laugh and laugh. Just a dose of silliness and laughter to start the day.

As we pulled up to school, I decided to park on the street in front of the school rather than pull into the congested parking lot. I did this occasionally as it made it easier to leave school and caused fewer interactions with the impatient and poorly-driving parents in the tiny school parking lot. As I parked along the curb, my daughter exuberantly and with the widest smile exclaimed, *"I put it in your brain, Mommy, and it worked!"*

I looked at her in the rearview mirror as I straightened out the car and asked, *"What worked?"* I was curious what miracle I achieved by simply parking the car.

"I wanted you to park on the street so we could walk through the trees to school and you did! You did what I put in your brain!"

I smiled. *"You put it in my brain?"*

As she jumped out of the car she yelled, *"Sure did!"* She was victorious and filled with so much joy at that moment. Her little brain decided it wanted to park on the street. It also decided to somehow pretend that she was landing that thought from her brain into my brain and when I did what she was hoping I would do, she was elated!

Such a simple moment triggered another amazing Soul Spark for me. I may not be able to engage in actual telepathy like my daughter believed she did, but if you believe in something, anything, and you put all of your energy towards it — big or small — it is bound to come true. Even something small as a parking spot.

Believing is just that. Taking what it is you want to create in your life, whatever intention that you set for yourself, and then wholeheartedly trusting not only that it could be true but that it is in this moment also true. At first this idea may feel unnatural, just like setting an intention or harnessing your manifestation superpower probably felt unnatural at first. But in time once you practice believing in whatever it is you want to believe in, suddenly you don't need to practice. It becomes natural. Everywhere you go and everything you do aligns with that belief, that vision, that intention that you are trying to manifest into your life.

So what did I do? I literally walked around shifting my mindset. Everyday, I would walk my daughter all the way to her classroom, give her a kiss and say *"Have a magical day."* She would always respond with a hurried *"Have a magical day too Mommy"*. She was eager to get inside the classroom and be with her friends as quickly as possible. Normally, the minute she was in her class I would reach into my purse and pull out my phone, staring head-down at whatever emails or texts awaited me. I would walk like this for 200 steps from the school to the coffee shop next door. Then I would keep staring at my phone as I waited in line to order my coffee (quick head lift to order, pay and make small chit-chat with the barista) and while I waited for my drink to be ready.

Then, I made a powerful shift in this morning routine. Instead of staring at my phone for the 200 steps from the school to the coffee shop, I started to use those 200 steps to believe. I used each of those steps to shift my thinking from whatever work or personal matter was pending and focus instead on deliberately believing. It wasn't just the walk to the coffee shop where I would do this but in any moment in my day when I was using braincells on something mundane — washing dishes, brushing my teeth, standing in line at the grocery store - I would consciously shift into focusing on my beliefs. Pretty soon I didn't have to remind myself to make these shifts. My regular day-to-day thoughts became consumed with these shifts, which meant that more of my day was filled with possibilities for my life — and that was exhilarating.

For me, I just started believing that I was living my most authentic life. I started believing that in every interaction, in every moment, in every conversation, that I was already the most real version of me. I decided this was how I was going to feel internally. I would consciously, actively, deliberately, intentionally be the truest version of me. If I forced myself to operate from that place, pretty soon I would just begin to feel it, honor it and truly be it on the inside. And if I could just tap into that feeling of belief, that feeling of knowingness of who I was and who I needed to be, then it was not only going to reside internally, it was going to radiate on the exterior.

I needed to put all my intentional energy into deliberately believing in what it is I wanted for myself and for my life. It wasn't going to be as quick and easy. It wasn't going to be second nature right away. It was going to take practice. But if I wanted to transform my life, if I wanted to create the life I'd only glimpsed, then I had to get to work. I had no other choice but to believe.

Hello Friend,

Just the fact that you are reading this book and you have stuck with it to this page means you are looking for ways to bring more into your life: love, money, stability, security, hope, passion, dreams, wishes, strength. Whatever you seek to add to your life, it is time to believe that everything you desire is not only possible but is ready to be unlocked.

The only way to get more of what you want is to believe that you already have it. It's about not giving energy to your self-doubt, to your critics, or even to the problems that may be consuming you. Instead it is about giving energy to whatever it is you wish to manifest. It is about knowing what you want to happen in your life and feeling in your bones that you already have what it takes to make it happen.

Try This Here is a simple way of experimenting with this idea. I want you to walk through your day hoping for someone to give you a cup of coffee. If you don't want a coffee, wish for a smile from a stranger, a free Slurpee at your local mini-market, or a parking spot right in front of your favorite store. Anything small and tangible will do. I want you to go through your entire day thinking about that coffee, smile, Slurpee, or parking spot. I want you to close your eyes and think about what it will feel like to have that small thing magically appear in your day. How will you feel when it happens? What emotions would it evoke for you? As you go through your day, I want you to repeat to yourself *that this thing you hope for has, in fact, happened. Say it to yourself. Write it down. Think about it constantly.*

Now it may not happen that same day and it may not appear exactly as you envisioned or hoped for but if you put your energy towards this simple thought, just see if you are able to attract it. And when you do, marvel in how good that small, simple coffee, smile, Slurpee, or parking spot popping up in your world makes you feel.

If it works for the small stuff, it will work for the big stuff too.

Always.
Me

CHAPTER 14

Hello Universe,

I have been contemplating so much of late and these journals have been a tremendous outlet to write about all that I am experiencing, all the mixed emotions, the confusions, the clarities. Having a place to express myself freely without judgment, to explore all the thoughts that are emerging has been such a blessing.

These journals have helped me to believe in my life and my intentions. They are my conduit to manifesting my best life. Writing is so healing. It makes me feel that my deepest heart's desires are not out there somewhere. But rather it is right here within me waiting to be unlocked, almost as if they already exist. More than all of that, it is making the idea of believing almost second nature. At first when I wrote about what I desired it felt unnatural. I felt like a fraud. But now, the more I write it the more it feels like the truth. An attainable reality that can and will come to be.

Always.
Me

I started journaling around the age of 12. I had the prettiest diary back in the '80s. It had a light blue cover and in the corner of each page where the loveliest little flowers and butterflies in perfect shades of pink. The diary even had a lock and tiny key. I was free to write my most private thoughts. As the eldest of three siblings, this was liberating. Writing about my daily 12-year-old angst was magical. I would find quiet spaces in our home, hide in the bathroom, or sneak out to the park and just write and write. Sometimes it was about how I wanted to change my name. Sometimes it was about how my parents didn't understand me. Other times it was about whatever tussle occurred at school.

October 1989

I miss our old house. My parents don't get it. But this house doesn't feel like home yet. I miss my old friends. My old school. My old neighborhood. Will this new space ever feel like home? I am guessing no.

Writing was a beautiful outlet that allowed me to keep moving forward while not getting stuck in any emotion or event that seemed too big to handle at the time.

I've kept a journal off and on since then, but in the years leading up to my 40th birthday it was mostly off. The stressors of family life, new motherhood, and my career didn't leave much time for myself to write or do much else. I was happy if I had time for an uninterrupted shower. Finding time to write would have been a downright luxury in those days. Then one day one of my favorite work friends came across a notebook at the hotel gift shop where she was vacationing and thought of me. She came back from her trip and gifted me this extraordinarily beautiful journal. The same sensation I had at age 12 with my first diary came over me now as I examined the exquisite cover and the extraordinarily beautiful pages. The journal was a work of art. I knew writing in it would be magical, but I had no idea quite how magical it would be and how the words that would eventually fill these pages would change the course of our lives.

At first, I wasn't sure what to write. It had been years since I engaged in any consistent practice. There were periods of time when I wrote daily, albeit just random thoughts. I had a blog for over a year — a great creative outlet. I even started a couple book projects, which kept me writing regularly for some time. Each of these writing episodes would enter my world, last for several months or even a year, and then gently give way to long gaps when I simply would not write. I would fall out of the rhythm of a daily writing practice and when I did, I unknowingly felt a void that I could not place. I now realize the void was not writing and not getting out onto the page all that was inside of me. Now with this new journal in my hand, I couldn't *not* write. I felt compelled to get words on the page and my breakdown presented the perfect opportunity to write daily for as long or as little as I liked.

The first day, I didn't know what to write. I just stared at the blank page for what felt like eternity. Rather than continuing to stare at the blank page, I finally decided that the most logical first step would be to write my name and the date. That seemed like an easy enough thing to do. As I wrote, inspiration hit. How about I craft each entry as a letter to my daughter? My scheduled breakdown was bound to be consequential. It would shift our lives in meaningful ways. It would be a time that she may want to better understand someday. Not only may this time period impact her life but also because the struggles I was experiencing could be experiences she too may struggle with when she is a grown woman. It seemed like the most natural way to proceed, so that is what I did. I started writing to my daughter daily.

The letters started out formal. I began with why I was writing, about when she was born, who her friends were. On the day of our anniversary, I wrote about our wedding. The entries started as stoic fact-telling. They later evolved. The entries became deeper and more reflective of the emotions, challenges, heartaches, and deep contemplations that consumed my consciousness. Slowly, rather than me telling my daughter in these letters about our day-to-day occurrences, each entry became more of a window into all that I was trying so desperately to make sense of in my life. Someday when my daughter reads these entries, she will see how hard this period of our lives was and how deeply I struggled with it all.

My commitment to journaling took on an almost ritualistic vibe. In the evenings, when my daughter was asleep and the house was quiet, I would retire to my bedroom. I would do my normal evening activities — into my cozy jammies, wash my face, brush my teeth. But to prepare myself to write and to connect with the Universe, I started to create an ambience that began my evening ritual. I would light my candles, sage my room, dim the lights, and say a prayer. I would fold my hands in front of my heart and thank the angels and spirit guides for this life. For all that I had, all that I enjoyed. For the family and friends who bolstered me up. For the job that I loved. For all the greatness that filled my life. I asked for my intentions to come to fruition. I would repeat them several times as if they were tiny mantras and in those few minutes, I would ask my whole body to believe they were true. I would ask my toes to believe it, my legs, my belly, my shoulders, my arms, my hands, my fingertips, my neck, my head. Tingles and sensation would fill my body. I was emitting an energy, a frequency a vibe of creation, of positivity, of heightened awareness, of love. And as I emanated this, I felt surrounded by beams of loving energy from the Universe. I would end by saying three *thank yous* to the Universe and slowly open my eyes.

I would cozy into bed, take my pen in hand, open the journal, and begin to write. Not only would I write the letters to my daughter, but I would also try to connect with the energy swirling around me. I would close my eyes and ask for an intuitive hit. I would literally put a question out into the Universe and ask for it to respond. Whatever I heard in those moments I would write down. I didn't question or try to make sense of it. I simply let the pen move and put onto paper whatever it was that the Universe sent my way. It was whatever presented itself in that moment. That was the hit. Once I was done releasing whatever words needed to come through me and onto the page, my evening wound to a close. I would put my headphones on, listen to soothing sounds and let the day go. The meditation, the prayers, the mantras, the writing — it was all the cozy blanket in which my entire being was wrapped while I slept. I allowed all those visions and thoughts to seep into my being and continue their manifestation and creation of my best life while I slept, blissfully unaware of the Universe doing its work.

Writing became a release. It became the way that I would transcend the day-to-day doldrums. It was the way all that was deep within me — all the confusion, the pain, the heartache, the struggles of my marriage that I was unable or unwilling to speak of — came out. It was an exercise in letting it all flow onto the page. All that I was feeling and all that I didn't even know I was feeling. All that was inside found a way out through the tip of my pen and onto the beautiful pages. Words, insights, connections. Thoughts I had never given attention to filtered onto the pages and into my ethos in a way that was liberating, freeing, and healing.

The experience was not just the act of writing or the ritual that surrounded it. The words on the page and their release from deep within gave energy to all that I was hoping to create in my life. I used the power of my words to approach all that I wanted. And while writing about my hopes, desires, and dreams felt unnatural, odd, or even uncomfortable at first, it slowly became the natural rhythm of my life.

Hello Friend,

The easiest way to lean into my beliefs and to manifest the life I desired was to write. I used journaling and the power of words to lean into all that I desired. Writing may feel perfectly natural for some and daunting for others. However, learning to let go of any fears around journaling and finding a way to frame it for yourself as a positive activity can unlock tremendous benefits.

Journaling does not require eloquent prose. Just flushing out onto paper all that is jumbling up in our minds, is one way we can clear the mental clutter and redirect our attention to all we wish to attract into our lives. Whether you write beautiful paragraphs, random sentences or words that don't make a whole lot of sense, the act of putting pen to paper is going to move you forward.

Try This

Let's start small. Take a journal or stationery of your choice. Write your name and perhaps the date on the first page. Close your eyes and take three deep breaths. Relax into this moment and be all in on this time to begin your journaling journey.

Whatever is within you, allow it to lovingly flow onto the paper. Pour out whatever needs to be released like a melody coming through your fingertips. If nothing is flowing, begin by just making notes of the thoughts that are coming to your mind. Do not worry about organizing your worlds or the style. Just let whatever you are hearing or feeling move onto the paper.

For some, the words will ooze out. For others, you may end up with fewer words. That is perfectly okay. When you feel like you have written all that you can. Put the writing away. Do not worry about what it means. Do not try and make sense of it. Resist the urge to organize the thoughts or make sense of them. Come back to your writing after some time — a few hours or maybe a few days. Consider what you have written. Thread it together. See if any insights surface for you. Also, congratulate yourself. You have taken the first step on what I hope becomes one of your healing practices.

Always.
Me

CHAPTER 15

Hello Universe,

In theory, I get that I should be grateful for everything in my life. But sometimes it's hard to focus on the good stuff when there is so much other noise around. The husband talking about his regular annoying topics. The chatter of friends and their meaningless gossip. My mother calling to complain about the landscaping in her community. The literal noise of the construction going on next door. Yet, I know if I am not grateful for what I have right now, You are probably (make that definitely) not going to deliver on all that I am hoping to manifest in my future. That's why I have also decided to incorporate gratitude into my evening rituals.

Each day I write down three unique things for which I am grateful. Not the same old stuff, but really trying to find unique things. I gotta tell you, when you have to come up with three things each day 1) it isn't easy at first and 2) it makes you traverse your day looking what you can write down. Surprisingly, the hunt creates a lovely change in the way you experience your days. I am more aware and present throughout my day and in turn that is making me more grateful. It is a wonderful shift!

And it's not only the journals. If I am really going to make gratitude part of my day, then I need to find multiple avenues to express it. I purchased a jar and each day my daughter and I write down things we are grateful for. We have made this part of our evening routine and it has become a wonderful way to experience gratitude together.

For this inspiration I thank you.

Always,
Me

Gratitude feels like the catchword of the day. Kinda like kale two years ago or quinoa a few years before that: something most of us never really knew before but now it has landed in pop culture as something we must love and embrace. Just as kale is everywhere — in our salads, in our smoothies, mixed into our favorite pastas — so is the concept of gratitude. I knew this word before, but it was just that. A word. It did not carry any depth of meaning for me and it most certainly did not have the cult-like following it now enjoys. These days gratitude seems to be on every coffee mug, t-shirt, and pencil you see. I never saw it as something I needed to practice. It wasn't something that I wanted to engage with. It was just a word.

These days if you are not actively engaged in practicing gratitude, you are likely to get booted right out of spirituality school. No guru, shaman, or spiritual practitioner of choice is going to take you seriously if you haven't taken the most basic step of moving yourself towards gratitude. And as annoying as something that shouldn't be trendy becoming trendy is, gratitude really is worth the hype. All those coffee cups can't be wrong.

If you look up *gratitude* in the dictionary, the definition is so simple. Yet when you sit with this meaning and incorporate it deeply into your life you realize the power of these simple words. Gratitude is *"the quality of being thankful; readiness to show appreciation for and show kindness."* It isn't a single act or a single emotion. It is the essence that emerges within you when you are feeling thankful, when you are feeling appreciation, and when you emanate kindness.

This is because gratitude is a stepping-stone on the path to manifesting the life you desire. It is perhaps the first way we can shift our experience within the Universe. Gratitude connects us to all moments, keeping us aware of what is happening and grounding us in the gratitude for all that is. It is worth its trending hashtag. It is worth the praise of the spiritualists. It is worth all the hype. It is most certainly worth your time.

Just like so much in my life, I realized that gratitude really did need to be practiced like yoga or riding a bike. The more you practice, the more it becomes routine. It becomes part of how you engage with yourself daily. It is not something you just throw out the window when it becomes less trendy. It is something that stays with you and becomes a part of you.

My gratitude practice started small. I would shut off the phone and all its notifications. I would get in a quiet spot where I knew I wouldn't be interrupted. I would just close my eyes and ask myself what I felt grateful for today. I would start by slowly rewinding my day and just remember the day's events a few seconds at a time. I recalled how I felt when I woke up, what I ate for breakfast, dropping my daughter at school, driving to work, conversations with co-workers, eating a delicious salad, laughing with my mom on the phone, making dinner, playing with my daughter, putting her to sleep. All the moments of my day, replayed like a highlight reel moment by moment. In so doing, one or two experiences lifted to the surface. Those highlights became the focus of my gratitude. Sometimes it was as simple as a beautiful sunset or a little drawing my daughter made at school. Keeping my eyes closed and my breath flowing evenly, I would focus in on whatever bubbled up for me. I would think about that moment and focus on the feelings it brought forth. The more I considered all the feelings or emotions that bit of gratitude brought up for me, the deeper my appreciation began to feel. I quickly came to realize that even in the worst days and worst moments, there is always, always, always something to hang on to. There is always something for which to be grateful.

To deepen my gratitude practice, I started setting the timer on my phone for two minutes to see if I could keep the feeling of gratitude going. During those two minutes, I would close my eyes and focus on one moment of the day. I focused my attention on that moment of gratitude to really feel all aspects of it. By thinking of these grateful moments intently for a defined period of time, I eventually learned to tune in all of my senses, all of my emotions, all of me on that feeling of gratitude and in so doing began to appreciate deeply so many happenings in my day.

Two minutes felt like forever at first. To think of all the reasons I was grateful for a simple moment — like the moment I devoured a slice of delicious chocolate lava cake after dinner — for two entire minutes almost felt excessive. Did the slice of cake require that much gratitude? But the more I practiced, the easier it became. Over time, I was able to ditch the timer and could hone in on gratitude with ease — not just superficially, but deep within myself. Kinda like doing crunches after years of not doing much exercise. You discover muscles you never knew existed (and after doing a set of 20, those muscles are burning!). It is similar with gratitude. The more your practice, the greater the depth of gratitude you will start to feel. When you go through your day knowing you will practice gratitude later, it forces you to experience each moment in your day differently. You look at the traffic jam, the noisy lady at the nail salon, and even the long line for the bathroom at a concert a little differently. No more short tempers. No more getting agitated. You just move into the moment and find the good in it.

Reaching that state takes time. It's a practice. You can't get good at your downward dog if you don't practice yoga regularly. You can't do the 10-mile bike ride without just getting on your bike and starting to pedal. It takes practice. It takes time. It takes commitment. Just like any other habit or skill that you are looking to add to your repertoire, gratitude requires careful practice. The more you do it, the more it will unlock all the positive resources of the Universe. The more you feel positive, the more you appreciate, the more you are grateful for, the more the Universe responds to your vibration and gives you more of what you seek.

Hello Friend,

Try This

I invite you to think of one positive occurrence — it can be big or small, significant or seemingly benign — that happened today. I want you to sit with whatever moment you have selected and intentionally, deliberately, be grateful for it. Appreciate that moment. Be fully aware of that moment. Can you relive that moment again with not just your eyes but all your senses? As you do, can you feel gratitude for that moment? Deep-seated appreciation and love for that moment. When you appreciate this moment, how do you feel? What emerges for you?

If you are anything like me, perhaps the intentional and deliberate practice of gratitude highlighted how much there is within our day-to-day lives to be grateful for. We live our days with blinders on to all that is good around us, all that we take for granted, all that we overlook.

When you start practicing gratitude, you find the glory in all the moments of your day. You start to experience your day through a different lens and when you do, the day becomes less a sequence of motions to get through but rather experiences to flow through.

Give it a try and see if you can make gratitude a regular part of your days.

Always,
Me

CHAPTER 16

Hello Universe,

Creating periods of silence in my regular life, no matter how small, allowed me to pause, re-center and stay connected with myself. Instead of reacting or lashing out, sitting in silence even for just a few moments each day allowed me to separate the big stuff from the small stuff. It allowed me to not react, but rather to respond. It gave me the time to be aware of whatever was coming up within me and to receive the precious insights that You landed in my awareness.

I learned that in that in silence life's answers slowly emerged. I just had to quiet myself enough to hear all that You were saying. I didn't need a psychic or an astrologer. I just needed myself and my connection to my own soul, which is what silence allows us to hear.

I love the way all these practices are blending and creating such powerful shifts. For all of this, I am so grateful.

Always.
Me

The world is so noisy. Every device in our lives has a sound — a beep, a buzz, a ring, a something. Watching the news is noisy. Not only do you try to hear what the TV anchor is saying, but if it is cable news, you hear the team of 10 so-called experts talk over each other as they explain why the latest headline should matter to you. Oh — and you do all of that while reading the scroll on the bottom of the screen about all that other news that those experts aren't even talking about. And don't forget the animation in the upper right-hand corner of the TV screen about whatever is coming up next. It is all just noise. Cable news, grocery stores, coffee shop and even dental offices. Every place is just buzzing, yapping, tapping, beeping away. As a society, we are accustomed to the noise. It is now the normal backdrop to the way we traverse our existence.

What if I told you all that background noise was stifling your connection with yourself? What if I told you that if you could tune out that noise and tune into the silence you would tune into your real self? You would tune into the Universe and all that it has to tell you. Would you believe me? Would you be willing to try?

I was no stranger to silence. I liked sitting in bed without watching TV. I liked going on a walk without my headphones on. I liked to sip my morning coffee quietly in the backyard. I liked the proverbial peace and quiet whenever I could get it. Yet being immersed in silence for days at a time, as I was when I went on my first silent retreat at Silent Stay, was a completely foreign experience. Allowing the silence to wash over me in that beautiful setting with the wonderful retreat leaders was an experience I will never forget.

If I close my eyes for just a quick second in my hurried days, I can virtually transport myself back there. Sitting on my favorite chair. It was next to the large windows overlooking the garden. That was the spot where my magic happened. I would sit down on the chair, place my journal on the tiny table for one. Each table had a small tealight candle and a matchbox carefully placed next to a small vase with a flower from the garden. I lit my candle and stared out the window and I would just be. Just lost in the moments unfolding outside in Mother Nature. The hummingbird zipping by, the water fountain slowing flowing drop after drop, the picturesque flowers with each petal to admire. And in that gazing, some moment of inspiration or insight would hit. I would open my journal and start writing. The pages would fill with the epiphany of the moment.

The depth of insight that I gained from tuning out the world and tuning into myself was unprecedented. I returned to Silent Stay a couple of times and the experience never disappoints. I referred to it as my spiritual tune-up to reconnect deeply, unleash more layers, and be washed with the silence. Sadly, Silent Stay burned down in the California wildfires of 2020. It was yet another reminder that I needed to create my own sacred silence in my everyday life to drown out the noise, to sit in silence and to connect for as long as I can, whenever I can. No one place can house our silence. We must find it within ourselves.

In a retreat setting, this is easy. The whole experience is designed to be noise-free. There are no TVs, no phones. You are one of six or seven people roaming over 25 acres. No city noises, no traffic jams. Just the sound of nature, our collective breath and the occasional sound of me dropping a book on the floor by accident.

At home, creating silence was far more difficult. Step One — shut off the TV. Seems simple and, surprisingly, it is. My husband kept the TV on constantly for background noise. He grew up in a large family and I think all that noise was comforting to him. As I shifted into greater silence, I would keep the TV off or stay far away from that noise if he was watching. It was yet another example of the distance growing between us.

Tuning out the background noises, whether it is the television, the microwave beeping, or your phone buzzing, is something I learned to do well with practice. In the months following my breakdown, rather than starting my days reaching for my phone and seeing what tragedy struck the world or what emails were sent while I slept, I kept the phone off. I made my morning coffee and sat outside on our deck. I just allowed myself to enjoy the coffee, the hummingbirds, the dragonflies, the slight wind, the fluttering leaves of plants in my garden, and soak it all in. I took one of my favorite reads, opened to a random page and allowed the words to linger in the air and in the silence. I let it all just slowly sink into the ether. I tried not to get carried away with some occurrence in my life. I just tried to be completely in the moment, allowing the soothing waves of silence to fill me before my household awakened and my mommy duties began.

As I did this, I also focused on observing. To be present in any moment means to see, to feel, and to experience the moment. When I first started to observe more, I did it intentionally. I took stock of each tiny thing around me to really see all that I was meant to see in this moment. That included looking and *really* observing a blade of grass — the shades of green, the shape, the way the light reflected on it and more. *Really* looking at the small flower that just sprung up — its shape, its color, its uniqueness.

I learned to observe and see more depth in every situation, every person, every object that came into my path. In line at the grocery store, driving in traffic, or just sitting in a meeting at the office. I saw situations more clearly. Why? Because I could immediately drop into being completely present and more fully see what was in plain sight.

Combining these two elements — the silence and the observation — is where the magic happens. When you drown out all the noise, all the extras that our life is filled with, really sit with the silence, that is when the messages or intuitive hits start to enter. That is where our connection to spirit, the Universe, God, a higher power, and even that innermost part of ourselves, is strong. That is when we are receiving. For any of our spiritual practices to work we must be ready to receive and create a space for the receiving to happen.

I heard best in silence. That is when my connection to the divine would power up. I was connected, I was aware and deeply in tune with everything around me. That is when I could slowly let go of the noise my mind created, the noise life created, the noise that just being human created. That was when I could recognize that all the thoughts, all the analysis, all the feelings, that really wasn't me. That was me in the physical body having a human experience. The real ME was the one observing the noise. The real ME was bigger than the physical me. The real ME pulsated around the physical me with an energy, a depth, a knowingness that is greater and larger than anything my physical self can explain. When I could sit behind the noise, that is when I could hear and receive.

The silence also provided enough distance that I could hear myself. Not the chatter of my mind and all the hyper-analyzing it wants to do. Instead, I could separate from that noise and sink into a deeper awareness, a better frequency to align with what the real Me, the spiritual Me, the soul Me, had to say. I could quite literally hear my soul speak. Being washed with this awareness anchored me to my innermost self, my spiritual self and less to external events, situations, circumstances, people, and objects. I was now anchored to Me and not to all the noise.

I created a life that incorporated as much silence and long stretches of solitude (at least so long as I could afford with a young child at home). I would sneak in the silence whenever I could. It mostly happened once my daughter slept in the evening and my husband was downstairs watching TV. My bedroom was already my hermitage away from the hermitage.

In these evening moments all my spiritual practices came together. It was when the downloads from the Universe became clearer. I already heard the Universe say that I needed to be my most authentic self. I already heard the Universe say that I needed to live a life of love. These intentions would, in turn, bring me close to what I wanted. Then one night in my silence I received the clearest of clear messages. *I wouldn't have to do a thing.* It was just going to happen. I didn't need to rush to meet a divorce attorney. I didn't need to pack up my things, pack up my daughter's things and run away. I didn't need to entertain any of the thoughts that would flood my mind when I felt I needed to act. Instead, I just needed to stay in the flow of the Universe. The Universe was slowly and carefully re-arranging the order of things so I could live my new life. I simply had to allow it to unfold.

Dear Friend,

I hear people say that they do their best thinking in the shower. Why? It's probably the only place that they are free of distraction. The only sound is the gushing water splashing onto your body. For you, it may be while driving or even while on a morning jog. It is the small window in your otherwise noisy day where silence exists for you. Even if that is your only place of solitude, I encourage you to use it.

Try This When I first learned to be more mindful and to be more present, one great suggestion I received was to observe each drop of water land on your nose in the shower. At first you think: how can I do that? I can never feel each drop. There is so much water coming at me! But if you try it, without question, without judgment, you will start to see that what looks at first as a big gush of water coming out of the shower head is just a bunch of tiny little drops and if you really try — quiet your mind, observe — you can feel many of those individual little drops on your nose.

Give it a go.

Always.
Me

CHAPTER 17

Hello Universe,

How did this happen? I am sitting in my closet shaking, trying to get the jumbled thoughts in my head out on to the page. My husband filed for divorce! He read my journals! He thinks I am infatuated with his friend! I can't even begin to put together what just happened. Is this real? I didn't think he was the type of person to rummage through my things! I didn't think he was the type of person to hire a big burly dude to pound on the windows of our living room and serve me with divorce papers while we both live in that house and while I was home alone with my daughter feeding her breakfast. Did that just happen?

These beautiful journals, my source of solace, my innermost thoughts, concerns, reflections, dreams. These sacred words were not meant to be in his hands. These words were not for his eyes. They were not for his complete misinterpretations. They were certainly not meant to make their way into court filings. These were my writings. My creations. My manifestations. My thoughts. My breakdown on these precious pages. They weren't for anyone, and they certainly were not for him.

Somehow even amidst the shock and confusion, I am still firmly in my flow. Rather than get angry, scream and yell over being served with divorce papers in the home I still share with him, I am sitting here in my closet as the words flow onto the page, realizing that this is the Universe taking action to move life forward in a scenario where I was completely unable to move myself forward.

Yes, I wanted a change. Yes, I knew my marriage was not serving me. But those realizations were just that. Realizations. I was a long way from taking any action. I wasn't brave enough. Universe, You were brave for me. You took the wheel. You reorganized the order of things to make what is meant to be happen. That intuitive hit I received a few nights ago when I was sitting in my evening silence was completely true! I wouldn't have to do a thing. I wouldn't have to act. You rearranged things to make happen what was meant to happen. And while the physical me didn't feel brave enough, strong enough, secure enough to take actions that would direct my life in the best possible way, You figured out how to put into motion what clearly needed to take place to allow me to be my most authentic self and to live a life of love and that starts with me being free of my marriage.

For this I am so grateful. A lot scared but a lot more grateful.

Always,
Me

I didn't see it playing out the way that it did. Even as I would visualize a new life, as I would ask for the Universe to show me the way, as I would hope for things to change, I had no idea, no inkling, and no download from the Universe that any of it would go the way it did. I didn't know that my husband was secretly recording my conversations with friends and family when he wasn't home, that he was reading my most private thoughts in my journal. I didn't know that it was him, not me, that would ultimately file for divorce. And I certainly had no idea that he would play victim, seek revenge, and make our divorce the most difficult and non-amicable situation of my life.

What I did know is that part of my spiritual practice was to sit with what is. I could have yelled, screamed, fought, argued, thrown something. But what I did instead was just be curious about what is. I strove to be above the noise of the day. I opted to just sit with what is and allow it to be.

This doesn't mean I never had moments of sadness, anger, and surprise. I had plenty of those. That is the human side of ourselves — and it is bound to come out because we are living a human experience. But I found that the deeper my spiritual practice became and the more rooted I was to something much larger than myself — spirit, soul, God, the greater awareness — that I could maintain my own deeper awareness, which wasn't tied to what people thought of me, or to what place I lived or what car I drove. My awareness was with the deeper part of me that knew whether he took the china or the fancy living-room chair or took more money than I thought he deserved, my identity, my life, and myself were not tied to any of those things. I was only tied to my inner awareness, my inner self, my inner sanctuary whose roots were deep and strong. It is my fundamental belief that this approach created an inner strength within me that continues to propel me forward.

Now, that doesn't mean that we never react. That doesn't mean that if we are in this spiritual realm that we don't cry, get sad, get mad, get angry. We do. That is the human part of us, and we accept that in these types of hard situations — like your husband filing for divorce — we are going to act human!

For me, that moment came as a big burly dude was pounding on my living room windows to serve me with divorce papers early in the morning while I gave my daughter breakfast. I heard a loud and jarring thud of someone banging on glass. I jumped up from the breakfast table, startled. A large man — bald head, leather jacket — stood waving a manila envelope. He kept pounding and shouted: *"Open the door."* I opened it slightly and the man shouted again: *"You've been served."* He dropped the envelope on my front porch and walked away. I stood still as I watched him walk towards his car and speed off. I slowly reached for the envelope. I took it in both hands. I had no idea who would serve me or why. I locked the door and walked back in, the sound of a man's fists pounding on my living room window still ringing in my ears. I opened the envelope to find divorce papers. I walked back to the kitchen table to my daughter's scared face. Even her little four-year-old self knew something was wrong.

Spiritualists talk about the idea of accepting and surrendering. It is the idea that you cannot internally stand in opposition to what is. When we cry, scream, punch, hit, lash out, we are physically fighting with what is happening. It's like being at battle with what is: fighting the reality, going to war with what is real and happening right now. Instead, if we accept what is, we are saying *yes* to this moment the way that it is. Not the way you wanted it. Not the way you dreamt it. But the way that it is in this very moment. You accept that and can feel some opening from within that says you are where you are. Sitting with that recognition and accepting it ultimately becomes your freedom.

Being served with divorce papers was scary and shocking. But what I also recognized almost instantaneously is that *it did* happen. It is what happened in that moment. In that moment, I was served with divorce papers. That was the reality. And when I accepted the situation and surrendered to what was happening, it was almost liberating. It was peaceful. It created a vast openness from within and a sense of knowing that this is the way the Universe created things to move my life forward. The Universe knew that while moving beyond the confines of this marriage is what I needed, I was incapable of acting. I was too gripped by fear. I didn't know what to do or how to do it. The Universe took the action for me.

And in accepting and surrendering to the way it all transpired, I was able to see within myself a dimension that is not dependent on external conditions nor on constantly fluctuating thoughts and emotions. I was not being jostled around anymore by a situation, a person, a place, or an event. Not even this divorce. It was not going to knock me off my center. It made me wobbly for sure. But I was accepting of what was. I used my evening rituals to be curious about it. I let go of my own inner resistance. I let go of my conditioning to fight, to control, to act.

It wasn't always easy. Once my husband finally moved out and my daughter spent her first night away from the only home she has ever known — trying to accept and surrender to that was not easy. It was crushing. It was devastating. I wept. I was overcome with a numbness as I experienced a depth of sadness that I had not known before. But even in my devastated state, I accepted the moment as it was. To move forward in our lives and to live outside the confines of this marriage made her shuffling between homes an unfortunate reality. I had no choice but to live with that. And to accept what everyone said: children are resilient, that at her age living in a two-home scenario would become completely normal, all that she ever knew.

What acceptance and surrendering does not mean is giving up. When you get a medical diagnosis for a terrible illness, you are shocked, sad, surprised, and unsure of what to do next. But to move forward, you must accept that you have this illness. It would not be wise to pretend the illness does not exist. It would not be wise to pretend the doctor did not give you terrible news. You must accept that this diagnosis is what is. But you don't just start writing your will and making funeral plans. You don't accept it and give up on living from that moment forward. The doctor probably gave you a treatment plan so you can combat the disease. You would be acting most prudently and in your best interest if you also accepted that treatment plan and did what was necessary to fight the disease. You accept and surrender to what is in the moment but that doesn't mean you don't have steps that are needed to make yourself better.

The same was true in my divorce. By accepting what is in each moment completely and in its entirety took me to more peace and helped me to see my situation more clearly. Fighting, yelling, lashing out — that wouldn't lead me to peace. Maybe I would feel like I got something off my chest. Maybe I would feel some sort of release. But what I realized is that for me none of that felt necessary. I needed to accept what is, even the elements I didn't like, if I was to be at peace.

I only got to this place through practice. I practiced, practiced, and practiced holding intentions. I practiced, practiced, practiced manifesting the life I desired. I practiced, practiced, practiced believing in all I could see for myself and for my future. I practiced, practiced, practiced gratitude. I practiced, practiced, practiced silencing the part of myself that doubted I could make the kind of changes I wished to see in my life. And I practiced, practiced, practiced sitting with what is, accepting it, surrendering to it but still knowing that I could stay in the rhythm of the Universe and keep taking steps to go where I needed and wanted to go. I practiced, practiced, practiced sitting with my inner awareness and being rooted to that rather than being rooted to any house, car, fancy purse or other external possession, person or situation. And through all that practicing, I raised my vibration and created the life I desired.

Hello Friend,

Have you ever had to accept a situation that you just didn't want to accept? Getting passed over for a promotion. Your boyfriend not proposing to you on that romantic vacation. Praying so hard for a medical treatment to work, but losing a loved one anyway. Or, in my case, your husband filing for divorce in a way you did not see coming.

Countless experiences in our lives are like this. We are humans living a human experience. But when our mind tells us to yell, scream, fight, flee, cry, experience deep anguish, hit, or even hurt ourselves or someone around us, does that feel good? Does that give you control? Maybe for a moment our mind tricks us into thinking those actions are ones of strength. But when we tie our actions to these emotions, what we do is just lower our vibrations. We lower ourselves.

If we are to lift ourselves up, we must be deeply rooted on the inside. We must restructure ourselves to recognize that outward negative reactions don't help us. To be in alignment with the Universe, sometimes we just need to sit with what is. Something did happen. We can't change what happened. We can have feelings about it. We can cry, feel sad or numb. But the real depth of our practice comes from staying aligned with what we know to be the truth inside of us. It is being aligned with our vibrations with a deep knowing that something greater than ourselves is at work. We align with this from a place of appreciation, love, and deep inner awareness.

To shift into this mindset, I suggest reciting the following mantra (or using this mantra as an inspiration to create your own).

"I am standing strong in this time, completely embracing all aspects of my situation, welcoming any shifts or inspiration that might come my way."

You may choose to use this mantra during your meditation practice, while you exercise, or on a drive. However, you choose to incorporate it is entirely up to you. As you repeat the mantra, really embrace each word and its meaning. Really feel the energy that speaking this mantra evokes within yourself. And as you do, allow yourself to feel whatever is emerging for you.

Always,
Me

HELLO UNIVERSE, IT'S ME

SECTION 3: LOVING ME
(AND HOW YOU CAN LOVE YOURSELF TOO)

CHAPTER 18

Hello Universe,

Today the divorce drama was intense. I couldn't take the stress, the sadness, the back-and-forth. On my way home, I pulled into the 7-Eleven parking lot a few blocks from my house and sobbed. I sat in my parked car and did an ugly, loud, sobbing, angry cry. I couldn't stop. I just kept going. My whole body heaved. My loneliness, my sadness, and the sheer stress of all that was happening was coming out in each tear, in each sob, in each scream.

Universe, I can't take much more of this. I can't handle it. Make it stop. I beg of You. If You were trying to break me in this process, congratulations — You succeeded. I am willing to accept my situation. I have used every spiritual tool in my toolbox and yet it all feels terrible. Just bring this all to a close. Please! Please! Please! I am sure there is some lesson in all of this, some way I am supposed to grow from this, but today, sobbing in my car, I didn't see a lesson. I didn't see a point. I am just exhausted. I beg You. Please make this end.

I never imagined divorce would be this contentious, this difficult, this painful. I never imagined the twists and turns it would take. I didn't imagine he would read my journals. I didn't imagine that he would file for divorce and then refuse to leave the house. I didn't imagine the legal shenanigans, the inability to reach any agreements and the animosity that plagued this process. My heart aches deeply in these painful moments. It aches for my small daughter who is living with this. It aches for what her future will hold and how to protect her. It aches of fear for all the unknowns that surround us. There is nothing left in me today to shoulder these aches. All I can do is cry and cry and cry.

Does this get any better? Am I capable of getting through this? Will going home feel like a torture chamber forever? Will he ever leave? Will there ever be peace?

I keep trusting in You, Universe, but on days like this You sure don't make it easy. Yet as I pulled down the visor in the car, looked at myself in the small mirror and tried to make my face look like I hadn't spent the last hour sobbing, I returned to what I know to be true. Universe, You got me this far. You got me to see that life could be different and maybe this really messy part is what I need to go through to get to the other side. But please, Universe, keep showing me the way. Give me some hope, some sign, that things will be okay. That this is all working out for the better. On days like this, I just can't see it. I just can't. But I keep trying. I know the only way to go is forward. I keep marching.

Always,
Me

Life doesn't just stop being life when we learn to meditate, sit in silence, have more gratitude. That doesn't stop the human experience. We may elevate our vibration by putting energy towards these positive and new methods, but that doesn't mean we no longer agonize over the pain of a terrible breakup, that we will never get in a car accident, or endure the trauma of a life-threatening disease. We are having a human experience — sometimes that experience includes frustrations, failures, and tragedies. It includes experiences that we cannot predict nor understand. It includes experiences that overwhelm us and seem senseless. It just does.

What can begin to shift as we move along our spiritual journey is how we respond to what is happening. My divorce-related drama lasted two years. There were multiple mediators, multiple sets of lawyers, court appearances, settlement offers, rejections, and even an unnecessary and very expensive trial — burning through money for no apparent rhyme or reason. Yet, it was during this period where my greatest spiritual growth occurred, where the greatest lessons of my life crystallized in the most beautiful of ways and where the shifts within myself were surprising even to me. The greatest distress of my existence led me to the greatest opening of my energy.

I started to see subtle shifts in my daily life. Instead of getting mad or yelling or letting a feeling of anger, resentment, hatred, or betrayal fester deep within me, letting it consume me and keeping me from sleeping at night, I responded differently. Not every time. But often enough. And when I did it was liberating. All the tools I equipped myself with were raising my vibration. I latched on to better energy and wasn't dragged down into the muck. As I raised myself more and more towards the good energy, I grew into the frequency where I could live a life that rejected the day to day noises choosing instead to tune into my truest self. I allowed myself to be guided forth by that energy.

My now-ex-husband and I lived in the same home for six months before he moved out, a contentious time when he filed for divorce and refused to leave the home. We already slept in separate bedrooms; that started months before the divorce started. The main change was that we did not speak to one another unless the topic related to our daughter. Every evening I would be upstairs doing my evening rituals — journaling, meditating, and manifesting. He would be downstairs plotting his next attack on me. Maybe it wasn't plotting. If I try to see it from his perspective, he too, was trying to make sense of this marriage that was unraveling. He wanted reasons. He wanted answers. He wanted someone to blame. Some explanation to hang on to. Maybe he just used the tools at his disposal (antagonizing me, refusing to leave the home) to try and extrapolate my thoughts, my motivations, my next steps. Perhaps it was part of his warped way of trying to get answers. But to me it felt like an attack. Every morning at 6AM I would come downstairs to make my coffee and every day he would confront me or try to antagonize me about some situation that had just occurred. This is how my mornings started every day for the longest six-month period of my life.

I naturally woke up around 6AM each morning. As my eyes opened, I whispered to myself, *"Thank you Universe, Thank you."* No matter how challenging and overwhelming life got, "thank you" were always the first words I released from my lips. It was a thank-you for this life, this breath, this experience. It was a simple way to show gratitude that no matter the circumstances, so much about this life deserved my appreciation. I rose slowly, brushed my teeth, went to the bathroom, and then as I approached the bedroom door, the moment I dreaded each morning was upon me. My daily challenge — to see if I could tiptoe down the stairs quietly enough to not wake the beast. Could I get downstairs, turn the water on to boil, get two scoops of my favorite coffee in the French Press, let it stand for about four, maybe five minutes, pour my coffee into my cup, add a splash of milk and tiptoe back upstairs to quietly enjoy my morning coffee before my daughter woke up and my mom duties commenced? And could I do this all without waking my husband and unleashing his morning onslaught?

I took a big inhale, gently placed my hand on the bedroom doorknob, closed my eyes and gave myself a quick 15-second pep talk. *You got this, Deepika. Today is the day! You can get down those stairs, get that coffee and be back upstairs without any confrontation. Goooooo team!* I slowly turned the knob. I carefully moved one foot in front of the other. I let my bare feet touch the beige shaggy carpet as gingerly as possible to minimize the sounds. Any squeak or thump on the floor would alert my husband that I was awake. I didn't want that. All I wanted was to drink my morning coffee in peace.

Nine times out of ten, as I slowly made my way down the stairs, the guest room door would open followed by the thud of my husband's feet on the hardwood floor as he rushed out of the guest room to start his battle. Nine times out of ten he was there before the water ever made it into the French Press. I wished I had a Keurig so coffeemaking would go faster.

This day was no different. The fourth step from the top squeaked. My heart sank. How I wished this step would cooperate. I tried placing my foot on different parts of it, but step number four always betrayed me. The squeak, however tiny, made it known that I was on my way down. The guest-room door opened. And so it began as it did on so many mornings.

These daily encounters were distressing not just because he engaged me before my first cup of coffee (which is a big no-no) but mostly because he knew specific details about what happened when he was not home: the details of conversations I had with my mom the night before; that a girlfriend came over when he wasn't home, and even what we discussed. He even knew the off-color joke my friend shared when she knew that I hadn't laughed in a long time. Was the house bugged? Was there a listening device? Was there a camera?

One day when my husband was not at home, my cousin Gary came over. We sat in the backyard enjoying the warm summer day. As our conversation went on, I confided that I suspected my husband was recording me, but I had no way of figuring it out. I didn't know what a listening device might look like and I certainly didn't know how to determine if it existed in the home. Gary, in his cool, youthful, and charming way, said, *"Well, let's find out."* We began a search. We went inside and communicated only through whispers. If our suspicions were right, we didn't want to be recorded while we were searching for the mystery recording device

We looked in every closet, every cabinet, in every drawer, underneath every piece of furniture, inside every vase, behind every painting, and even took a flashlight to look up the chimney. We unscrewed every electrical socket, every light fixture, and every vent. We scoured the entire home and came up empty. The only place we didn't examine was the guest bedroom, which was now the ex's abode. We became convinced if some type of listening device existed, it had to be in there.

Gary and I needed a reason to walk into that room. If we were being recorded, then it needed to look like we entered the room with some purpose that wasn't to locate the mysterious listening device. We whispered up a plan. Gary would walk into the room under the guise of getting the extra pillows out of the closet so he could take them to his new apartment. He needed extra pillows. We had extra pillows. They just happened to be in that room.

We put away our whisper voices and standing outside the room used our overly-animated regular voices. I went first. *"Hey there, Gary! There are extra pillows in the downstairs bedroom closet. Why don't you take those?"* Gary responded with, *"Great idea. Can I go grab them?"* I ever so cheerfully replied, *"Well, of course you can!"* Our acting skills were terrible, but it worked. He opened the door, walked straight to the closet, opened it, grabbed the two pillows off the shelf, walked out and closed the door. The whole episode took 15 seconds but in those 15 seconds we saw a camera perched right next to the door. It was on and recording. Suspicion confirmed.

All these months I was going crazy trying to figure out how my ex knew what he knew and now I understood. When he left the house, he turned his camera on. In the evening he would listen. Then every morning, he would confront me with his latest detective work. To say that I was devastated, shocked, and surprised is an understatement. Even though I didn't want to be married to this guy, even though we were in divorce proceedings, I never imagined he could or would stoop so low as to not only read my journals but also to record me in our own home.

Over time, it was almost comical to contemplate what golden nugget of information he would be compelled to confront me with next. *Oh, so you think you can hide money from me? You think I won't figure out what is in the bank account? Where is all your jewelry? Where did you put it? You know I can locate it, right? You know I have ways of doing this. Oh, so your Mom thinks it's okay to poke fun at me? She thinks you will get remarried someday. Who would marry you when they find out what you are like? Oh, and you think my friend is interested in you? That guy is my brother. What would he do with you? You think I will move out? I am not leaving here until I get what I want from you. You will have to pay up.*

A normal first instinct in such situations would be to attack right back and make this showdown a two-way affair. I could snoop on him, too. I could go through his things. I could follow him and see where he went, what he did, who he was interacting with. At the very least I could speak up and try and defend myself from his attacks. *Well, you drink too much. You are spying on me. I know about your listening devices. And where is all your money? What are you hiding? I pay 100% of the bills around here — the mortgage, the utilities, the groceries. Where does your money go? No one is poking fun at you. Do you think my Mom wants to see her daughter's marriage fall apart? And why are you so worried about what my mom, my friends or your friends think anyways? Do you get that none of that even matters? What matters is the absurdity of the situation we are living in?*

But that was not for me. I learned to focus on making my coffee and not reacting to him. He would start talking and I would let him talk. I wouldn't engage. I wouldn't respond. He would unload about whatever hurtful topic he could conjure up overnight. I learned to merely say, *"Thank you for your comments. I am going to drink my coffee now,"* and walk back upstairs to my bedroom where I could have my coffee far away from him. I did not want to engage with him. I didn't want to fight. I didn't want to give him the satisfaction of seeing him get a rise out of me. I just rose above his noise and walked away. This doesn't mean that I wasn't frustrated, angry, hurt. It doesn't mean that his words and actions were not deeply distressing. It doesn't mean that my stress levels were not through the roof. They were! I am human, after all. I was mad. I was upset. I was stressed in ways words cannot fully describe. His attacks were piercing.

His words and blatant misinterpretations were not my truth. Just because he chose to say what he said did not make it real. My husband had become my external saboteur. He was trying to spew whatever he could my direction to break me, to make me think less of myself, to make me doubt myself.

Instead, I choose to keep faith in my own internal knowingness, my own awareness, my own truth. I focused on my manifestations, my journaling, my meditating, on receiving the intuitive hits and being on the lookout for the Soul Sparks that appeared, no matter how small, even in the darkest moments. I kept believing that the life I desired was around the corner. That no matter what he said or how difficult he made the situation, soon enough this part would pass and the next part of my life would be ushered in. That next part would be extraordinary. How did I know? I believed it to be so. I was growing into my manifestations each day to create the life I desired I had to keep going through this to get to where I was meant to be.

I lived in the present moment. I maintained my awareness, kept connected to my source (my higher power, the divine, the Universe, God), and kept my clarity and in so doing kept my sanity too, which was not easy to do when for six months you are cohabitating with someone who filed for divorce, refusing to leave and now recording you daily. It is insanity-inducing. But in the now, in the present moment, him shouting, talking, intimidating, spewing his conspiracy theories didn't matter. In this moment, he was only talking — and I was walking in my truth. Leaving those conversations with a *"thank you for your thoughts"* rather than a fight elevated me. It infuriated him but it elevated me. I made a conscious choice not to engage because in my present moment I felt no need to. No benefit would be derived from it. That was my truth and I was determined to live it. Over time, it became almost fun to see him lose it over how little his attacks impacted me.

Now, this doesn't mean that his attacks did not arouse something in me. It surely did. There were days where I would cry over the madness of it all. I would vent it out with my friends and family. And there are a few times where the frustrations got so overwhelming that I did get mad and I did fight back. *Stop! Stop! I've had enough of you and your lies. Stop this madness. What are you trying to accomplish here? What are you hoping I will say? Just get away from me. Take your lies and your half-truths and keep feeding them to your friends. I am sick of the BS. Stop it!* But most of the time I focused on shifting my mindset and choosing to not allow those feelings of anger or frustration to guide me. I choose to let it work differently within me. And when I did, I lifted myself up in magical ways.

Whenever any of us are in these type of terrible situations, the feelings that emerge within us and then fester are all tied to our own fears *The last time someone fought with me, I didn't argue back and that made me feel small. I am going to argue this time because I don't want to feel small again.* Or the terrible feeling bubbling up now is related to a future fear. *If I cry, sob, and beg right now, maybe he won't leave me. I don't want to be alone at age 40. Maybe I can just try and make him love me?*

Whatever feeling emerges, know this — in this very moment you can choose to rise above all of this and just be in the glorious, the beautiful, the amazing present. Don't spin on the old stuff and don't spin on the stuff that hasn't happened. Just be here in this moment.

And in this moment you are whole, you are complete, you are protected, you are under the care of the divine and it really doesn't matter what craziness someone throws at you. That is on them and not on you.

It also doesn't mean that we don't reflect or ask why these triggers arise. We do. We also know that the hurts, the pains, or the triumphs of your past have created the current version of you. But right now, in this moment you are in the present. And in this moment, you can choose to just be. You can choose to rise above the noise, the chatter, the arguing and just know that you are elevating yourself each time you respond in a way that you couldn't even imagine doing before. Learning to live in the now and having the realization that in this moment, I am okay, I am safe, I am strong and I can handle what may come my way. I can handle the fears that are bubbling up — *Will my daughter adjust? What will people say? How will I be perceived? Am I going to be strong enough to start over?* These fears were real and valid. But the ability to move through those fears and being able to strongly and safely land on the other side was priceless.

It's priceless to learn to hold back on contemplating life until you're ready to tackle it. Sure, we want to know why certain situations keep occurring. We want to better understand how these experiences shape this moment. But spinning on that thought constantly just brings the chaos to new heights. Add to that the "bundle effect" of throwing all your past fears and hurts into the current pain. It creates an avalanche of emotions that feels unsurmountable. Instead, I worked to not tie everything together. I learned to take this moment for what it is and release any past experiences or future implications from it. When I did that, I was able to examine and understand the current circumstances for what they are.

I also learned not to spin on the situation in the moment I was triggered. Whenever I felt triggered, I would sit in the awareness of feeling triggered and tell myself that I understood how I was feeling and that we would explore this feeling more fully when I am in a time and space to allow myself to go there. For me, that was during my evening quiet times. Examining whatever emotions are rising up for a time when you are free to unravel them, rather than in the moment the emotion spins to the surface, creates a necessary separation that allows us to live in the present while recognizing further healing work needs to take place.

Hello Friend,

Have you ever gotten in a heated argument? You remember not having the right words or perhaps spewing out all the wrong ones. You remember the way the argument felt like someone had punched you in the stomach and how you didn't know what else to say or do. You remember storming off, slamming a door, or throwing something. And if you are anything like me, you remember sitting in your closet and crying over the madness of it all.

These fights take everything out of us and leave us feeling terrible whether we were in the right or the wrong. I want you to know that there is a place for anger. You are allowed to be angry. There is nothing wrong with these feelings. But what if we found a way to de-escalate our heated emotions and give them some space.

Try This *Speak to your anger. Have a conversation with the anger. Try and approach the anger as if it were a person in your life. You can quite literally say "Oh, hi, anger. I see you are here again." You can ask the anger, "What is triggering you today?" "Why is this pain surfacing today?" Comfort this part of you with words like "I understand you feel this way. I really do." In conversing with the anger, you humanize it, you recognize it, and by talking to the angry place inside of you, you will be able to slowly change the way this feeling emerges for you and potentially deter the escalation that so often occurs.*

You accept that the anger is there. You don't avoid it. You slowly learn to handle the anger better by acknowledging it and engaging with it in a different way. But if the anger is simply too much to bear, it is okay to reach out to a friend, a therapist, a professional who can provide more tailored insight on how to address that triggers you.

Learning to embrace and understand our anger can transform the way we flow through our life experiences. Give it a try.

Always,
Me

CHAPTER 19

Hello Universe,

*I am so much better at being curious now than ever before.
I only have You to thank for that. These days, I am open to
what is happening around me without questioning, without
judging, without high amounts of analytical gymnastics. I can
just allow things to unfold and I remain open and curious as
to what is happening. When I questioned, judged, or analyzed
everything, I was paralyzed. I just couldn't stop! That was not
only exhausting but it was fruitless. All it did was spin me in a
continuous loop of worry and stress.*

*What I know now is that we must stay curious and open
to all that unfolds. This is why I know — like, I know — that
everything going on in my life right now is exactly as it is
meant to be. I know that You listened to my intentions and
that You orchestrate everything so my intentions manifest
in the best possible way. While it may look different than the
picture in my head or may not take place on my preferred
timeline, I know that it is all designed to yield the very best
outcome. I promise to allow myself to be open to the way
things are unfolding. When steps happen that are different
than I anticipated, I am going to do my best to be open and*

curious as to why it is emerging in this way.

I never would have gotten to this place without receiving your messages and keeping me in your flow. For that, I thank you.

Always,
Me

In order to maintain my spiritual mindset, one quality became key: Curiosity. The act of remaining curious — of continuing to explore, discover, being eager to know became central to my spirit.

As my divorce unfolded, there were good days and there were downright terrible days. I started viewing my day-to-day more as a flowing river. I wasn't interested in what others thought of my story. I wasn't interested in how I appeared to others. I wasn't even interested in how each individual scene played out. Instead, I was focused on staying in my flow. As situations presented themselves, I viewed them as rocks in the water. I was curious why they appeared, and I wondered about the impact they may have, but I kept myself grounded to keep flowing along. I didn't let the next incident, the next terrible occurrence, the next surprising twist throw me off. I just tried to stay in my flow. Even when the situation took a turn I did not envision, I stayed open and curious as to why it happened the way it did. I did not tie myself to any particular outcome. I focused instead on being open to receiving what I desired and knowing that it may be packaged in a way I couldn't have possibly envisioned.

There were days when I would wallow in self-pity. I would feel that the latest twist of events was not one I could bear. I would get myself into a temporary tizzy and revert to all those old ways of handling a bad situation that seemed to land in my lap — eating ice cream, crying, yelling, feeling like the world was out to get me. But I didn't let myself sit in that space for long. I gave myself grace that I reverted to that space for whatever period of time. But I always picked myself up and stayed on the path of being curious and open to why a circumstance was unfolding the way it did.

As I sat with this openness and this curiosity, I rooted even further into my spiritual practice. I rooted even further into my belief that the Universe always delivers. And every time, literally every time, it did.

This curiosity played itself out on a beautiful sunny day as I walked into our couples' therapy appointment. As our relationship soured, he became insistent on going to counseling. This was surprising given his lack of interest in therapy the countless times I mentioned it during our marriage.

We both drove separately to these appointments so I could rush off to work afterwards and he could head to the small business that we owned. On this day, I walked in feeling good. I typically dreaded these sessions, but today I felt a little hopeful, not because the sessions were going well or helping us connect. Far from it. We were more disconnected than ever. But on this day, I felt like a shift was in the air. I was positive, hopeful, encouraged even, not by any particular action or event but just an overwhelming energy was brewing that felt good.

As the session got started, we both sat down on the couch, me on one end and my husband on the other. As we were about to begin, I looked over at his face. He stared stoically at the therapist. We were only sitting a few feet apart, but it felt like the Pacific Ocean was between us. We were each so disconnected, disinterested, and genuinely dispassionate about the other. Yet as I looked at him, He seemed so handsome, even lovable in that moment. I felt some softness towards him, some hope, some sensation deep down that maybe his intentions were pure and that we could correct course. I wondered occasionally how much my husband knew about all the spiritual concepts I was grappling with. He knew my time off had something to do with self-discovery, but he had no idea what truths I was uncovering. Or so I thought.

Within minutes, I realized that the Universe was once again creating the situations and circumstances necessary to move our story forward. The therapist asked who wanted to start, who had something to say. He said, *"I do."* He launched into a lengthy, rambling intro. I didn't know where he was headed. Eventually he got to the point. My lack of interest in him was because I planned to run off with his friend Dave. He went into excessive detail about why he believed this to be true. As his diatribe continued, I looked out the window. The trees swayed gently with the wind as beautiful rays of sunshine hit each leaf. I vacillated between watching what was happening in the therapist's office, listening to my husband go on and on, and staring out the window. I knew this was a moment I was meant to be curious about. I didn't understand why he was saying these things or how he got these ideas in his head. I didn't know what he hoped to accomplish with these misinterpretations. What I did know was that this was all unfolding. This was the present.

When he was done talking, the therapist asked me how I wanted to respond. I took a long pause, not because I didn't know what to say, but because I didn't think this audience would understand it. The truth was Dave came into our world to spin it around and to set the course for changes that would take place. That completely unknowingly, and without any intent, Dave was moving our story forward. Even now, as Dave sat thousands of miles away, he was doing the Universe's work some six months after he last visited or had any contact with us.

Instead of that truth, I took a deep breath and settled for saying, *"You have it all wrong. This is not true. Where are you getting this from?"* I then said that Dave was a nice guy, a smart guy, and someone I have liked and enjoyed for as long as I knew my husband. There was much to admire about him, but I hadn't spoken to Dave since he last visited — and I certainly had no plans to run off anywhere and do anything with anyone. But that is where I left it. I didn't think the audience could absorb much more.

The bigger mystery for me in that moment was how my husband drew these conclusions. I should have realized right then that he was reading my journals, but I was too unwilling to believe that could be within the realm of possibilities. Yet it was true. How else did he know about the Cowboy? To escape my reality and imagine the life I desired, I created a boyfriend who I named the Cowboy. I wrote about him in my journal. The Cowboy was 75% George Clooney (the only celebrity I have ever loved with all my heart) and 25% other men in my life who I dated, obsessed over, loved, or admired.

One night while sitting in silence and meditating, I had a vision of myself metaphorically putting all these men in a blender, whipping them up to create the Cowboy. The Cowboy was the man that I would escape to when I closed my eyes or felt a need to daydream. The Cowboy was the embodiment of the person I wanted to be with. He was the person I wanted to live my life with, the person with whom I could be my truest self. It was the person that loved me for all of me — the fine lines on my face, the flabby arms, the stretch marks on the tummy, the C-section scar. The Cowboy was the perfect doting partner who lifted me up rather than brought me down. The Cowboy and I were spiritually connected. The Cowboy was my alternative Universe.

He wasn't any one person. It wasn't Dave. It wasn't George Clooney (although George, if you are reading this, I am single so give me a ring, will ya?). The Cowboy was a make-believe lover, friend, confidante, boyfriend, husband, persona who was my escape. He was not an infatuation, a love, or a desire to end up with any one specific person. He was just the place I went to in my head. He was my emotional outlet as I manifested, dreamed, believed life could be different.

They also wouldn't possibly understand how much I resented having to create a fictitious character — an alternative reality — just to survive the day-to-day of my marriage. *Why couldn't this all just BE better? Why couldn't this just BE what I needed it to be? Why do I have to imagine someone else?* Yet I also believe that the Cowboy was created to show me a new path. The path that allowed me to see — finally see — that I could be me, I could realize my fullest potential, I could honor my truths and that someone would love all of me without reservation. Plus, who wouldn't want a cowboy that looked like George Clooney to appear every time you closed your eyes?

Yet in that moment, I knew neither the therapist nor my husband would be able to understand this truth. I didn't need my husband, the therapist, or anyone else to understand it. It was the way I was coping and what I was doing to keep moving in my life. I just sat there like the river, continuing to flow despite this bump being presented in my way. I remained curious as to why this had just transpired and what it all meant, but I was firmly rooted in continuing to flow where the current took me.

Hello Friend,

When was the last time you really stayed curious? Instead of getting frustrated or flustered, you opted for a feeling of curiosity and openness to what was occurring. If you have never managed to do this, just know that you are not alone. In our society we are conditioned to respond with a sense of right versus wrong or good versus evil. We have seen countless TV shows, and movies where confrontation, frustration, anger, and outburst are the norm.

We can, and should, make a shift from these types of responses to a response that is more measured, open and curious. For me, it helps to see a situation as an outsider, as if I am watching it play out as a scene in a movie. Using this lens, I can more easily see how an alternative response or reaction may have benefited me and those around me.

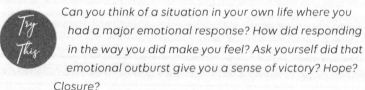 Can you think of a situation in your own life where you had a major emotional response? How did responding in the way you did make you feel? Ask yourself did that emotional outburst give you a sense of victory? Hope? Closure?

Now try extracting yourself from the situation and look at the same place, the same people, the same circumstances, as if you were watching it play out on a screen. Watch it as an outside observer. Do you see anything different? Do you see how you may have been able to respond in another way? If you reacted differently, how does that feel for you? What *would you want your character in the movie to know? What would you want your character to understand or consider before she finds herself in the next scene?*

Stepping away from our emotional responses and being able to look at situations from a space of openness and curiosity may unravel for you other emotions, thoughts or shifts that help with your own personal spiritual journey. Give this a try the next time a situation occurs that impacts your flow.

Always,
Me

HELLO UNIVERSE, IT'S ME

CHAPTER 20

Hello Universe,

I love when more people who understand the spiritual side of me appear in my life. You have been dropping people into my world to help me shift into a new way of thinking for some time now and as I continue along this path, I enjoy these new faces more and more. I love having these people with whom I can share experiences and insights.

Not everyone can accept new ways of living. Yet everything in our world constantly changes. Leaves change from barren in the winter to lush and green by spring. Why can't the way we experience the world changes, too?

I have learned this lesson firsthand. I went from a high-powered, analytical, organized taskmaster trying to control and manage a gazillion things all at once to now living much more in the flow of the here and now. I don't sit in the lotus position meditating all day. I still have that high-pressure job. I still have my family and multiple things to manage. But I just try to move through all my responsibilities and daily activities with a deeper connection to myself and the energies around me. Connecting with others who experience the world similarly has kept me moving forward in miraculous ways.

Please keep bringing these friendships into my life. They are opening my eyes and keeping me on my path. For that I am so grateful.

Always,
Me

When you start shifting into something new, you begin to meet people who also embrace similar things. If you get serious about fitness, then you suddenly encounter more people engaged in these types of activities. If you start to become more outdoorsy, you will come across others who share this passion. The same is true with spirituality. The same people with whom you connected over a glass of wine about breakups or heartaches may suddenly also have a spiritual side to them that you never knew before. Or, if you are reading this book at a cafe, someone may approach you to discuss what you are reading. In some way or another, as you move on your unique evolutionary path, you are bound to discover others with an interest in the same things as you. I refer to these people as my Spirit Pals.

My Spirit Pals appeared in plain sight. I didn't know Lilly, a younger woman I worked with for several years, was grappling with the same issues as me. She and I worked together on some of our company's most important clients. We would talk multiple times a day about work-related topics, but also managed to find time for fun and light-hearted conversations over lunch or at Happy Hour with our other colleagues.

Lilly and I were working late, finalizing a presentation for a major client meeting the following morning. When we were done, I said something like, *"Okay, Universe: make this a good meeting for us."* Not something I would typically say in work mode. I never wanted to expose my thoughts about the Universe to my colleagues. I was still very much grappling with what all this meant. I caught myself as the words were coming out of my mouth and thought, *why on earth did I say that? My colleague is going to think I am off my rocker.* Much to my surprise, she responded quickly without hesitating, *"Oh, we got this. All the signs have been lining up for weeks. Universe is gonna make it so."* We both laughed, ended our call. I realized that I had just uncovered a new Spirit Pal.

The next time we met, we talked openly about this. Turned out she, too, was exploring her more spiritual side. We ended up quite literally comparing notes, and for the last five years she has been an integral part of my spiritual growth and I of hers. We discuss our insights and delve into deep spiritual thoughts on a regular basis. Having Lilly's support to explore these spiritual pursuits has been such a gift.

Or take Ria, a friend for more than 10 years. We always had a natural connection and regularly discussed all sorts of typical girlfriend topics with ease — shopping, dating, traveling, families, careers. Slowly our conversations evolved from business ideas and relationships to spiritual topics. Ria was a yoga and meditation teacher, so we always connected around how to deepen our meditation practice. But one night when speaking of meditation, Ria slowly cleared her throat and very hesitantly shared *"Today, as I left the house to come here, I felt compelled to run back in and grab my tarot cards. Shall we pull a card? I am getting the feeling that Universe has a message for us."* Even though we were close friends and shared so much over the years, in that moment she was cautious in revealing her more spiritual practices. I looked at her with a big smile and said *"Abso-fucking-lootly."* We shared a big laugh. I didn't know much about tarot cards, but in that moment, we gave ourselves permission to share our spiritual sides more freely. Our evening moved into a realm of otherworldliness and our conversations have never been the same since. Ria is a great Spirit Pal because no insight is too small, too big, or too abstract for us to want to ponder together. Knowing that she understands my journey and that I understand hers has led to a connection that keeps the two of us flowing forward.

As you explore the more spiritual side of yourself, find the people who will support you in that process. It may not be your mom or your partner. They may not get it at all and think you have fallen off the deep end. That's okay.

There will be people in your life who are very important to you and who you are very close to that are not considering all that you are now wondering about. Doesn't mean those people don't remain your friends or that they don't remain important contributors in your life. What it does mean, instead, is that there will be people drawn to you and people that you are drawn to that will help you on your spiritual journey. There may be people you are yet to encounter or even people who are right there with you in plain sight that you never knew contemplated the same topics that you are now considering. Having the support of others will allow your experience to deepen in magical ways. And in time, elevating your spirituality may just rub off on the least expected people in your life.

Hello Friend,

Do you belong to a particular community? A community of parents at your child's school, a yoga studio you frequent or even a book club? Every time you see people in your community, how do you feel? For most, when a sense of community exists there is a fellowship around shared beliefs, experiences, or interests.

As you move deeper through your practices, you will see that finding a special place or person to explore your spiritual side deepens the experience. These places or people will show parts of yourself you haven't contemplated before and in so doing provide powerful teaching moments that deepen your own spiritual practices.

Try This You may even know of someone you wish to discuss these topics with. If you came across someone that you felt had Spirit Pal potential and you wanted to approach them, how would you strike up that conversation? Think of three questions you could ask this person and what their responses might be. Being prepared for the conversation wherever it strikes — in an elevator, at a party, in line at the grocery store — whenever it strikes, could help you find a powerful Spirit Pal that moves your journey forward. And remember, there is nothing for you to be afraid of in approaching someone. It is safe for you to open yourself up. It is yet another part of the journey.

Always.
Me

CHAPTER 21

Hello Universe,

My friend called today. She extended a simple and completely innocent invitation to go out and have some fun. Yet, I was completely taken aback — and I said no. It's not like I never go out. I do leave the house to work. I go to my daughter's school when I drop her off and pick her up. I go to the coffee shop. I go to the grocery store. But since the divorce, I find myself much more insular. I don't want to talk to people outside my intimate circle of confidantes. I certainly do not want to inadvertently bump into someone at the shopping mall or at the park. I have no desire whatsoever to post any updates on any social media sites. My only desire these days is to embrace my private persona and be more deliberate about who I interact with and why.

But in being more private, I can't help but wonder if I am hiding. I mean I have no reason to hide, right? I have done nothing wrong and even if I had there is still no reason to hide. I don't need to abandon or avoid every person I once knew because I don't want to talk about my divorce. I don't have to do that. And while I know that this is true at some level, I am still actively avoiding people. Why?

Why am I not wanting to talk about my divorce, my struggles, my pain? Why am I avoiding speaking to those people who have been pillars of support for me at various times in my life? Now I am literally ghosting them.

This Soul Spark has certainly given me something to be curious about. You always deliver the Soul Sparks when I need them most. And I hope in the days that come, You will shed more light on this one.

Always,
Me

It was a warm and sunny Saturday, and my daughter was with her father. I sat on a lounge chair by our pool. I didn't like to swim even though I took years of lessons as a kid, but I loved sitting by the pool in my swimsuit, soaking in the sun and reading a good book. I was relieved that our divorce was largely behind us. Our daughter had transitioned to a two-home system as well as could be expected. As with everything in our divorce, there were bumps on that road too.

There were many nights my daughter would refuse to sleep at her Dad's house until she could FaceTime with me so I could help her with her prayers or softly sing her to sleep. Knowing that it took her crying and screaming for her Dad to agree to call me was painful. He never told me that she was crying and upset, but I could see it in her eyes, the way only a mother can, that she was relieved through her tears to see me and provide the comfort in that moment that she needed. But slowly, and I mean very slooooowwwwwllllyyy, we all settled into our new normal. I knew she loved her Dad and her Dad loved her. They had fun together and there was little, over time, that I needed to worry about when she was in her Dad's care.

The phone rang. It was Sara. She was one of the few friends in my life who knew the details of my situation. In her happiest of voices Sara said, *"Let's go out tonight and have some fun."*

"Fun, what's that?" I replied sarcastically. Honestly, in that moment I could not recall the last time I went out to a fancy restaurant, had a long hard laugh with a friend, or danced a night away. It must have been years since I went out with a group of friends and just let loose. I told Sara that I was okay being home and that if she wanted to come over to my place, she was more than

welcome. She said, *"Come on! Why not go out and just have some fun? Don't you deserve to have some fun?"*

And that is when it hit me in the way Soul Sparks always do. The world slowed down. Suddenly, all I could see were the letters F-U-N hanging in the air over the pool. From somewhere deep within myself a sudden emotion bubbled up. I was living with a deeply rooted belief that *I was not deserving of fun.* This belief chose to make itself known through my friend's simple invitation to go out and enjoy ourselves for an evening. It had probably been affecting me for years and years — yet I was completely unaware. But here it was now, coming to the surface. I was not deserving of fun. I started to see every time that I avoided situations, people, parties, text messages from friends, relatives, former confidantes. I did so because I didn't want to engage. I didn't want them to see what was really going on.

Why was I undeserving of fun? Where was this all coming from? I realized that buried deep within myself was the belief that I had failed. Divorcing made me a failure. Not having a good marriage made me a failure. Subjecting my child to two homes made me a failure. Being divorced was something to be ashamed of — and even if I wasn't ashamed, I certainly should not be proud. It was something to hide. It wasn't something to talk about. And if this big part of my life was to be hidden away, then I couldn't be out and about enjoying myself. I just didn't deserve it.

As I sat with this, my eyes filled up and the tears started to flow. I felt incredible sadness that this feeling was inside of me and that it unconsciously shaped my life. Through the tears, I became more and more curious about it. *Why did it start? When did it start? Why would I hold on to such a falsehood about my life and myself?* But most importantly, I accepted this feeling and in almost the same moment, I also committed to breaking free of it. My life had been limited enough by a marriage that did not work and by the messy and protracted divorce that followed. Ten years of my life were tied up with this person and a relationship that did not allow me to be who I needed to be. No more. Not only was I deserving of fun, I was deserving of being open about my life's story, about what happened, to share it — and to share it unapologetically.

Trying to live a more spiritually oriented life didn't make me immune to toxic thoughts. It didn't block me from lies that had chosen to make my mind and body their home. My new way of being gave me the awareness to see all that was shaping my present and all that needed to be healed. Accepting all of ourselves, even the parts we don't like or would prefer didn't exist, is another element in growing spiritually. We must face the truths, even the hard ones, and work through them.

Hello Friend,

As your spiritual practices grows, you may better understand the limiting beliefs you've previously held and the impact it had on your life. I give you this space to start the process of releasing these limiting beliefs and allow yourself to experience your present circumstances without all that old baggage.

I prepared this mantra for you to help in this process:

I release any previous experience with this limiting belief and invite all of what is needed to create my life as I imagined it.

Repeat it as many times as feels comfortable. You may choose to write it down and re-read it each day. As you do, really feel this mantra within yourself. Feel what it will be like when you truly release whatever limiting belief is holding you back. And feel the power, the grace, the upliftment, the courage of letting this belief go so you can instead invite into your life whatever is needed to create the life you desire.

To deepen this mantra, you may try tailoring it to be more specific to your unique situation. Simply fill in the blanks. I fully let go of _____(enter the limiting belief here) and open myself up to_____ (enter the experience you prefer to have in your life).

Give it a try.

Always,
Me

CHAPTER 22

Hello Universe,

I hadn't had a night like that in years. My friend did not take no for an answer and eventually I acquiesced. I dolled myself up. I put on my fun clothes. I curled my hair. I did my makeup. I wore my high heels. Took out my fancy purse and off we went. I enjoyed a cocktail. We had a great meal. We laughed. Those kind of big belly laughs where your stomach hurts from laughing and where your eyes water from the hilarity of it all. And we danced! There was a band playing. We got up, hit the floor, and danced. I forgot how good it feels to dance and dance and dance.

I realize how hesitant I was to go out and face the world. Then You reminded me in the most wonderful of ways that having fun, being happy, enjoying and just letting loose is just as important as all those other spiritual practices that I have spent the last few years incorporating into my life. Having fun is fun! I needed that.

Always,
Me

I spent the previous two years actively culling my environment from the very wide net that I once had — overflowing with family, friends, extended friends, work colleagues, commitments, overcommitments — to one far smaller and more deliberate. I created an existence where only what I wanted was present. I deliberately, intentionally, unabashedly created a cocoon of sorts where I was wrapped up with everything I wanted and nothing else.

Now I was ready to spread my wings. I didn't want to hide from people. I didn't want to avoid them. I had no reason for shame. To really be in my truth was to accept it — and that required not being afraid of being judged. People say what they are going to say. Let them. Their words are their own. Let them just be that rock in your flowing river. A tiny bump, but you keep flowing.

Part of that flowing meant allowing myself to be seen. To meet friends again. To share my story. To hear theirs. I stopped hiding. I stopped avoiding phone calls. If someone was wanting to connect with me, I no longer avoided them. I took that phone call. I responded to that text. I went to that family party and I held my head up high. And — perhaps most healing — I shared. Not with everyone, but with those who did care, who were concerned, who genuinely wanted to know and understand my journey over the past two years, I shared. There is great healing in that.

There is also great healing in having compassion for ourselves. I realized that my scheduled breakdown was an act of self-compassion. I engaged in heavy self-care, introspection, and fun as a way of giving myself the warmest embrace. As a way of saying loudly and to all of myself that I loved me. That I hadn't forgotten about me. That I was there for me. That I cared for me. Yet as the revelations started to pile in one after the other, I felt sad that I was responsible for creating all the situations that I now found myself in. Part of me even felt mad that I let myself get to this point.

I tried to replace the sadness and anger with compassion. I tried to treat myself as I would any other friend going through a tough time. I wrote myself a letter using the same words and phrases that I would say to someone else in my situation. In this letter, I did something that I didn't expect. I forgave myself. While I was the one with the lesson to learn in my life and in my marriage, I forgave myself for not honoring my truest self in my relationship. I forgave myself for living a life that did not represent my most authentic self. I forgave myself for forgetting about me and not making myself more important.

I also forgave my ex. None of this was his fault. He may have done and said many things that diminished my light, but I let him and that is all on me. This was my journey, my self-discovery, my soul that was locked away banging on the door trying to be heard. To harbor any anger, ill will or acrimonious sentiment was a fool's errand. I forgave all of it and I continued to forgive. And as I did the weight of all the burden, sadness, pain that these years were filled with began to lift away.

Hello Friend,

Fun isn't always about dancing the night away. We can have so much fun right in our homes if we try. Licking the icing off our fingers as we eat cupcakes. That's fun! Trying new eye makeup. That's fun! Dressing up in fancy clothes with no place to go. That's fun! Putting my headphones on, turning up the music and having a solo dance party. That's fun! There are simple, inexpensive, and highly enjoyable ways that we can have fun. And well, fun is fun.

Fun is also an important act of self-compassion. It is healing and expansive. We can balance all the toughness that life brings by finding ways to enjoy ourselves. As we enjoy, we expand into a space that lovingly moves us forward.

Moving ourselves forward is also supported through forgiveness. Being able to forgive ourselves and others is the ultimate act of self-compassion. Unfortunately, most of us cannot instantly forgive. We have to practice forgiveness each day and little by little move in the direction of releasing whatever pain, resentment or sadness in order to love ourselves more fully.

Try This

Write yourself a letter of forgiveness. You may choose to write to your current, past or future self. In this letter release whatever is within you that needs to be forgiven. Perhaps it is the need to forgive yourself for a wrong done to you as a child. Perhaps it is a need to forgive yourself for being in a relationship that did not serve *you. You may want to use your letter to forgive someone else who hurt you, minimized your worth or just made you feel deep sadness. Allowing yourself to write this letter freely and openly will be a first step in practicing forgiveness and a huge step in engaging in greater self-compassion.*

If you are anything like me, not every step of our journey was thoughtful, wonderful or perfectly executed. But we can recognize the parts of ourselves or of others that were not great, not nice, not operating to support our highest selves and work to forgive. We can practice forgiveness of ourselves and of others and as we do we can keep moving ourselves forward.

Give it a try.

Always.
Me

CHAPTER 23

Hello Universe,

*I woke up early this morning, made my coffee and sat in
the backyard. The roses were in full bloom and their scent
lingered, pairing with the long jasmine hedge covering the
entire length of the back fence with its bright green leaves
and pristine white and purple flowers. I heard the birds
chirping, saw the butterflies fluttering.*

*I was immersed in the energy of the moment. The energy
was pure love. Each mesmerizing scent, each chirp, each
hum, even the sound of the morning traffic in the distance,
the brightness of the morning sun, the way the clouds were
streaking through the sky. This moment emanated love and it
felt like it was curated just for me. All the highs, lows, sadness,
joys, heartaches, and revelations that filled the last two years
all got me to this point. All the upheaval, all the tuning into
my innermost self, all the times I was vibing high, not getting
sucked into the drama, all the times I cried in my closet, all the
times I poured my heart out onto the pages of my journals,
all the paintings, all the silence, all the mediating, all of it, it
was the ultimate act of love. Each step was guiding me to
me. To love me. To pick me. To get back on the frequency that*

let me move my life forward. All of it was an act of love and in this moment, in my backyard, the roses, the jasmine, the butterflies, the birds, the sunshine, all of it was descending down from the heavens the most glorious energy. The energy was wrapped around me in what felt like the biggest, the most loving, the most jubilant of hugs. I did it. Not only did I do it, not only did I survive it, not only did I make it to the other side, but I did so with love.

For this, I am so incredibly grateful.

Always,
Me

I was committed. I practiced daily. The journaling, the meditating, the manifesting, the believing, the gratitude, and the silence. That daily practice kept elevating my vibration and kept shifting me further into the life I was meant to experience. It was an evolution. It didn't just happen one time and *poof,* I'd mastered it.

This is not something you conquer or master. It is something you continue to experience throughout your remaining years. It is the one relationship that, once discovered, is truly meant to last a lifetime.

And just like any long-term relationship, the nature of the relationship may change. One technique or method may work exceedingly well for you, then fall flat and no longer resonate. That is okay. You will find a new method, a new angle, a new way. Your practice is ever-evolving. As you grow, as your experiences change, as the circumstances of your life change, you will find differing ways to enhance it. You may have started with evening walks as your way of connecting with your deeper self and falling into your silence. It may now not be an evening walk that resonates, but something completely and totally unexpected. Something we cannot even contemplate in this moment.

For me, the methods have largely stayed the same. My evening ritual is still to light my candles, sage my space, write in my journal, define my intentions, believe in them, to meditate, to be grateful, to sit in silence, to receive. What has evolved in this process is the depth and understanding that I gleaned from all that I do. I see more shifts. I see more synchronicities. I notice more depth and meaning from outwardly trivial things. In my quietest moments, washed in the silence, sitting with my awareness, I receive all the Universe wishes to bestow.

My practice has led me to one fundamental truth. That if we are anchored in our awareness we will not be rattled by external situations, people, circumstances, or objects. Whenever life happens around us, we see it for what it is and stay connected to our core. When that happens, it is magic.

Hello Friend,

Whatever your place in life — be that physical, emotional, mental, geographical — whatever is pulling you in whatever direction, just know that you are the captain of your ship. You aren't being dragged through the mud, you are not just a robot that has been lulled into doing things the same way each day. You are in charge of this existence, your place in it, how you navigate through it and even the direction you wish to head. It is all within you. Go where you are meant to go. Live your life as you wish to live. Let yourself be who you are. Show yourself to people. Share your truths. Dance your dance. Stop holding back. Don't be cautious. Just unfold before the Universe. Universe created you to show all of you. So show yourself unabashedly, authentically, completely. Be in the flow of this existence and know as you do, to walk in your ultimate truth. When you do, it really is magic.

Always.
Me

EPILOGUE

Dear You,

I am incredibly proud of you. Look how far you have come. Look how much you are seeing today that you never saw before. You are blessed. Your family loved you, raised you, taught you about hard work and determination. You took all that your family ingrained in you and worked so hard excelling at school and at work. You should be so proud of your achievements.

But then why, after such depths of love in your upbringing and such confidence in your academic and professional life, did you betray yourself? Why did you settle for so much less than you deserved in your personal life? Why did you stay in that loveless, lifeless marriage for so long? I tried to steer you each step of the way but I knew for you to see, really see this life, I had to let you discover all you were meant to about yourself in these experiences. You learned the hard way. And while it was painful, and while there was heartache, and while there was so much you had to trudge through, you made it. You are on the other side. And look at you now.

Look how aware you are of life. Look how much you can see in each day. Look how grateful you are today for things you took for granted before. Look how much the love within you has expanded. Look at the greatness in your life. Not the titles or the bank accounts, but the greatness within you. You have unlocked so much of what your soul needed to. You feel the energies of this magical universe and you now vibrate with them. Marvel in that.

Yet there is more to learn and experience. Life may not always be smooth. You will have bumps. You will have barriers. You will have upsets. Some will be small. Some will be large. That is life. But with whatever life brings your way, know that I am with you. Know that if you stay in your newfound awareness, your newfound knowingness, your newfound harmony, you will be able to navigate whatever realities you face. While you are here now and here is a wonder, there will be a tomorrow. Whatever that tomorrow, that new moment, that new experience presents, just keep coming back to this time in your life when you got to the other side. Bask in the knowingness that you made it to the other side of this large life episode far better than who you were when you entered it. You are right now the very best version of you. You are filled with light, with love, with magic.

Everything you need to keep unlocking more of yourself, continuing to see the depth of love within yourself, to see the magic of your existence, is all sitting within you in this very moment. Each new experience will keep showing you this more and more. Trust in the process. Always know that I am here. I am listening. I am sending you beams of love and strength. You can always see me.

Just keep our connection strong. Whether it is sitting in silence, being in nature, meditating, journaling, or whatever new way you discover. Stay connected to me and I will be connected to you always. All is well and all will continue to be well.

You are so loved. Feel that love within you and beam it out to others too. And always remember to marvel in it all.

Love always,
The Universe

ACKNOWLEDGMENTS

On my 40th birthday, I restarted a journaling practice. As my pen first graced the page of my beautiful new journal, a deep inner knowing washed over me that these journals would one day be the foundation for a writing project. Little did I know back then, that writing project would be *Hello Universe, It's Me.*

To my **daughter**, my greatest heartfelt gratitude goes to you. Restarting my journaling practice as letters to you, launched a journey that changed our lives. It is my hope that when you are a grown, mature woman, with life complexities and experiences all your own, my words provide meaningful reflection and understanding. You are brave, courageous and the absolute joy of my life. Your spirit, your energy, your being inspires and motivates me in ways that I am still uncovering. Thank you for being you and selecting me as your Mom on this journey of life.

My life journey started under the loving care of my parents. Thank you for braving the immigrant experience twice – first to Canada and then to America – to give your kids the very best. It was a perfect upbringing. For all the hard work, for all the struggles, for all the values you instilled in me, and for that magical love that surrounded me each and every day, I thank you.

To my **Dad**, thank you for being the original girl dad well before it was a trending hashtag. For believing in your kids, for making us laugh with your jokes and for waking us up early – soooooooooo early - on the weekends with your singing. You cherished every second with us in this life. Maybe at some level you knew, as I feared, your life would be short. I loved every moment with you, even your early morning incessant singing, but especially the magical way you made me believe I could be anything. The love we shared still fills me to this day and for that I am incredibly grateful.

Mom, thank you for being the epitome of beauty, brains and grace. Thank you for teaching us through your example, that even when life gives you lemons you put your lipstick on, fix your hair and make lemonade. Thank you for being by my side always with your unwavering support. Knowing you are always there means more than I can express.

For every lifetime I endure on this earthly terrain, I hope my brother is always by my side. **Mehtab** your balanced and honest perspective is what makes you incredible. Thank you for all of your support, guidance and love through all of my life's decisions big and small. A special thank you for demanding I walk back into Crate & Barrel and buy that pink velvet bed because, as you so eloquently stated, if I want a giant, pink, ridiculously expensive bed after all I have been through then I should march back in there and get it. Oh and a special thank you for creating your own incredible family for my daughter and I to love.

If you ask my sister about our relationship growing up, she would tell you that it was akin to Marsha and Jan in the Brady Bunch. A lot of "Marsha, Marsha, Marsha." Well **Puneet** you better write your own book quick or it will continue. Just kidding. The truth is, I always felt in your shadow. You are brilliant beyond measure, levelheaded and always the most diplomatic soul. Being your sister is a blessing. Knowing you would listen, knowing you cared, knowing you love my daughter as if she were your own gives me great joy. Don't even get me started on how much I love the little people you brought into this world.

If anyone needs the ultimate friend, confidante and a pillar of support, look no further than **Sheena**. For all the laughs and all the cries, for all the ups and all the downs, for all the inspiration and intuition, there is no one I would want in my corner more than you. Your unlikely friendship has been a gift.

The night Princess Diana died we lost a Princess, but I gained friend. I had no idea that night sitting in your dorm room (because you were the one with a TV) watching the breaking news of Princess Diana's death that **Mindi**, would one day be my very best friend. We have shared so much – boyfriends, heartaches, the deaths of our fathers, Zoom game nights during Covid and more. Through it all I could always count on your honest and thoughtful perspective. You were always there to listen. You were always there to help. A thousand thank yous for being you and letting me always be me.

This book would not be here without my incredible editor **Allison Landa**. For believing in this project, for pushing me to add more scenes and dialogue when I didn't think I had the ability to add anything else, for all the cheerleading and encouragement, I thank you. Your insights and perspectives took this book where it was meant to go and for that I am grateful.

To the design and marketing team at **Little Men Roaring** for always entertaining my crazy ideas and translating them into something far better than I could imagine, I thank you. I am so grateful for your contributions to this effort and your immense patience as I learned the ropes.

Finally, to my colleagues at **Connor Group**. For the flexibility, the support, the patience and the friendship as I traversed the most difficult period of my life, I thank you. In my worst moments of sadness and despair, I know I was a terrible co-worker. I let my life drama overwhelm my days and impact my work. Thank you for giving me grace as I evolved into my new normal and landed on the other side. And a special thank you to my colleague and friend **Maisha**, who gifted me an exquisite journal that would change the trajectory of my life forever. Maisha, for the role you played in sparking the writing I thank you.

Printed in Great Britain
by Amazon

32076994R00136